DARD HUNTER THE GRAPHIC WORKS

by

Lawrence Kreisman

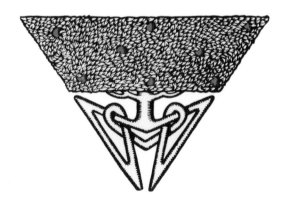

Pomegranate

SAN FRANCISCO

Published by Pomegranate Communications, Inc.
Box 808022, Petaluma CA 94975
800 227 1428 • www.pomegranate.com

Pomegranate Europe Ltd.
Unit 1, Heathcote Business Centre, Hurlbutt Road
Warwick, Warwickshire CV34 6TD, UK
[+44] 0 1926 430111 • sales@pomeurope.co.uk

Front cover: Adaptation of Dard Hunter's 1905 cover design for *Nature* by Ralph Waldo Emerson (page 68).

Back cover: Dard Hunter, design for a window in the Roycroft Inn (page 97).

Library of Congress Cataloging-in-Publication Data
Kreisman, Lawrence.
 Dard Hunter : the graphic works / Lawrence Kreisman.
   p. cm.
 Includes bibliographical references and index.
 ISBN 978-0-7649-6185-4 (hardcover)
 1. Hunter, Dard, 1883–1966—Themes, motives. I. Hunter, Dard, 1883–1966. II. Title.
 NK1412.H86K74 2012
 745.4092—dc23
                     2011040203

Pomegranate Catalog No. A204

Designed by Patrice Morris

Printed in China

21 20 19 18 17 16 15 14 13 12   10 9 8 7 6 5 4 3 2 1

Contents

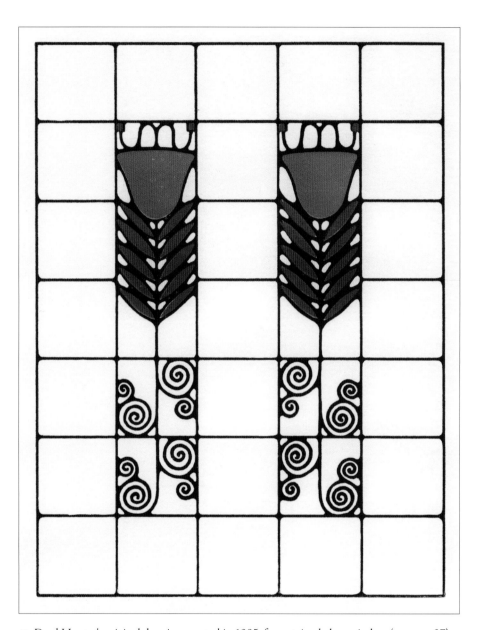

■ Dard Hunter's original drawing, created in 1905, for a stained glass window (see page 97).

Acknowledgments

I AM INDEBTED to three generations of Hunters for their documentation of life and work in autobiography, biography, and stewardship and preservation of important documents. I am also grateful to the groundbreaking biography by Cathleen Baker.

A number of talented people with experience in and understanding of the Arts and Crafts movement, the Austrian and German Secession, and the book arts have taken the time to encourage this publication through their careful review of several drafts and/or their suggestions for inclusion of materials that add depth to this colorful period of Dard Hunter's life. These include Bruce Smith, Wayne Dodge, Glenn Mason, Dr. Graham Dry, Cathleen Baker, and Dard Hunter III. I am grateful to all of them for their comments in support of this publication. Pomegranate Communications' publisher, Katie Burke, gave me the freedom to expand upon the original planned parameters of the book. Stephanie King, associate publisher, and Rachel Anderson, managing editor, provided effective and thoughtful comments during the editing process. Dard Hunter III shared family photographs and the remarkable graphic legacy of his father and grandfather at Mountain House. Eileen Wallace located these archival materials and prepared the images for publication. Finally, designer Patrice Morris thoughtfully assembled text and images into a beautiful volume, which truly showcases early twentieth-century graphic design.

■ Dard's self-portrait advertising his School of Handicraft in the April 1909 issue of *The Philistine* is based on a drawing made to look like a wood engraving, from a photograph by Clara Ragna Johnson (figure 1).

Introduction

YOU OFTEN FALL IN LOVE with something without really knowing why—it speaks to you, and the dialogue continues to enrich your life whether or not you figure out some logical reason why it occurs.

For me, picking up a book from Elbert Hubbard's Roycroft Press has that effect. The first response is a sensual one—the limp suede leather binding caresses the fingers and encourages inspection. But the true treasure lies inside, from the uneven surfaces and edges of handmade papers to the illuminated cover page with stylized designs to the complex initials that begin chapters and sections.

I have loved and collected books for years but was drawn to the Roycroft books not so much by the bindings—a number of contemporary publishers did similar work—as by the remarkable graphic imagery and experimental typefaces by Dard Hunter that lay between the covers.

Dard Hunter excelled as a designer, craftsman, printer, typographer, and papermaker. While a near contemporary of such progressive graphic designers as Boston poster and typeface genius Will Bradley, English-born New York artist and illustrator Louis Rhead, San Francisco Bay Area artists Arthur and Lucia Mathews, and publisher Paul Elder, he nonetheless forged his own design path. It would be hard to find another American graphic artist whose work compares.

My initial attraction to Hunter's work is now understandable, for I was drawn to the designs of artists and craftspeople from the German and Austrian Secession. So was Dard Hunter. How did a youth growing up in Ohio tap into such a progressive source of ideas, make them his own, and succeed in giving these designs national exposure? The expression "The stars were aligned" seems appropriate to the tale.

1 Portrait of Dard Hunter at Roycroft by Clara Ragna Johnson, a photographer at the Roycroft shops who later made her home with Dard's family in Ohio.

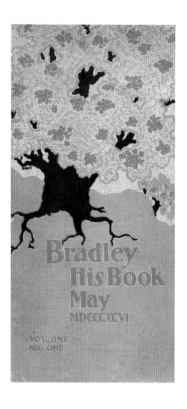

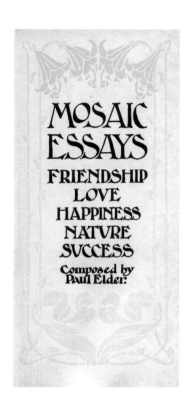

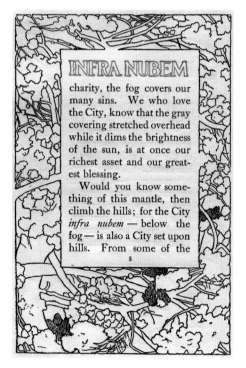

Clockwise from top left:

2 *Bradley, His Book* (cover), vol. 1, no. 1 (May 1896),
Wayside Press, Springfield, Massachusetts, illustration
by Will Bradley.

3 "The Night-Blooming Cereus," poem by Harriet Monroe,
in *Bradley, His Book*, ibid., illustration by Will Bradley.

4 Frontispiece, *Mosaic Essays*, composed by Paul Elder,
Tomoye Press, San Francisco, 1906.

5 *Infra Nubem* (one of three essays; the others are *The
Lights Outside* and *La Bocana*) by Alexander McAdie,
Philopolis Series, A. M. Robertson, San Francisco, 1909,
decorations by Lucia K. Mathews, frontispiece by
Arthur F. Mathews.

Images courtesy Dodge/Kreisman Collection.

It was kismet that he grew to maturity during the last years of the nineteenth century and the first decade of the twentieth—when the design community was questioning its traditional role, the relative place of handmade versus machine-made processes, and the products that could be made available at home and abroad. Artists and artisans were opening themselves to experimentation that was often at odds with the status quo.

Dard Hunter questioned the designs he was exposed to and sought to explore new and different ideas overseas rather than simply follow in the footsteps of the accepted theories at home.

It was his good fortune, and ours, that he was mentored in Elbert Hubbard's Roycroft shops, where personal initiative and creativity were appreciated and workers were given permission, time, and even monies to experiment and bring back to the workshops the knowledge they gleaned from these experiences. In Hubbard's library of British and European design periodicals, Hunter found his muse in such periodicals as *International Studio* (the American reprinting of the British design monthly), *Dekorative Kunst*, *Deutsche Kunst und Dekoration*, and *Dekorative Vorbilder*.

6 Left: *The Studio*, vol. 1, 1893, had a cover designed by Walter Crane; the message "Use and Beauty" was taken up as the mantra of the Arts and Crafts movement.

7 Right: *Deutsche Kunst und Dekoration*, vol. 8 (cloth binding) (April–September 1901).

Images courtesy Dodge/Kreisman Collection.

Had Hunter connected himself with a more rigid, less open-minded businessman, his curiosity and follow-up might have been stifled. And had he been with a publisher who lacked the extraordinary entrepreneurial genius and marketing abilities of Elbert Hubbard, several years' worth of remarkable graphic designs would have been seen by only a very small number of Americans.

Hubbard was immensely popular. His regularly issued magazines and essays—including *The Philistine*, *The Fra*, and *Little Journeys*—as well as scores of books, catalogs, pamphlets, and mottoes, were distributed around the country by mail, sold in fine gift stores and department stores, and subscribed to by many libraries. As a result, Hunter's work entered the homes of thousands of Americans of every income and social level. Even after he left Roycroft, his designs continued to be used by Hubbard and his son in new and reprinted books through the 1920s.

Hunter's most important contribution to American graphic arts was his success at adapting contemporary European avant-garde design ideas into a graphic design vocabulary that was made available to the mainstream. It is unlikely that most readers of the Roycroft books had any understanding of the British, Scottish, German, or Austrian designs that had inspired Hunter. For that matter, not much has changed in a century. Most casual browsers today would not directly identify his work with this brief but defining moment when modernism was present in myriad forms in many countries.

My longtime friend and colleague Dr. Graham Dry, a British-born art historian and lover of books who has spent much of his working life in the auction houses of Munich, recently shared his perspective on the extent to which Dard Hunter's designs borrowed from specific German or Austrian designers' work:

> You cannot really ever mistake Dard Hunter for the genuine Viennese thing. He was a borrower naturally, but out of respect and admiration, not to cut corners or to conceal a lack of imagination, and thoroughly inventive with all that came his way. He was very careful about not copying directly and I can always sense his own style though based on British Arts and Crafts, Glasgow School, Austrian and German Secession design and the work of Will Bradley. It is altogether a very successful mixture and a very genuine and unmistakable original American style.[1]

The life and work of Dard Hunter have been well documented. In 1958 his autobiography, *My Life with Paper*, an expanded version of his *Before Life Began* (Rowfant Club, 1941), was published by Alfred A. Knopf, which had published his groundbreaking study, *Papermaking: The History and Technique of an Ancient Craft* (1942).

To reintroduce Dard Hunter's creative output to a community that largely associated him with his later contributions to papermaking by hand, his son Dard Hunter II prepared *The Life Work of Dard Hunter*. This beautiful and painstakingly assembled handpress work covered the two clearly distinct periods of his father's career. Produced as a limited edition (150 copies), the two-volume work resides in libraries and private collections.

Volume 1, completed in 1981, reviewed his early life and influences: the graphic design period during which he lived and worked at the Roycroft campus starting in 1904, the periods in 1908 and 1910 when he lived and studied in Vienna, and his short residence in London during 1911–1912.[2] Dard II estimated that his father designed and saw through the press more than one hundred books and pamphlets. It is interesting to note that in his later years, Dard himself regarded these with enmity and even went so far as to use the term "mortifying."[3]

The second volume, completed in 1983, described the part of his father's work for which he is better known today. Dard Hunter became the leading collector, scholar, and proponent of handmade papers. According to Dard II, his father was the first person in the history of bookmaking to have produced by hand a complete book including the paper, type, and printing. By the end of his life he had produced eighteen volumes on the subject of paper-making by hand.[4]

8 Dard Hunter II at the press, 1949.

Grandson Dard Hunter III has restimulated national interest in and appreciation for the graphic work by making remaining prints from Volume 1 available to the public, establishing a website (www.dardhunter.com, which includes a brief history of Dard Hunter's career and his achievements in graphics, type, and papermaking), and marketing type fonts and products that incorporate the designs.

Cathleen Baker completed an outstanding biography, *By His Own Labor: The Biography of Dard Hunter* (Oak Knoll Press, 2000), after years of organizing thousands of letters and documents at Mountain House, the Hunter family home in Chillicothe, Ohio, and spending research time at Roycroft and in Vienna. For those who wish to learn more about Dard Hunter, these collected works are wonderful resources.

I do not intend to go into detail on the personal and family life of Dard Hunter except as it relates in some way to influences that clearly played a role in his maturity as an artist, an artisan, and a printer. Nor does this book focus attention on the second career he forged as the foremost authority on handmade paper. It showcases his growth as a graphic artist and the beautifully crafted and intelligent designs he created. It questions how Dard's design work

9 Mountain House, c. 1900.

reflected contemporary graphic design and how he broke away from what others were doing as he was influenced more strongly by the work of his European counterparts. While this book is not intended as a facsimile of Dard II's Volume 1, it does follow the chronological layout and includes some of his commentary and analysis of his father's artwork, along with Cathleen Baker's insights and my own evaluation.

This publication reveals the beauty, variety, and character-defining forms and typography that distinguish Dard Hunter's work from that of others. Many people, regardless of their knowledge of design history, can recognize his work and call out a "Dard Hunter rose" wherever it appears. Dard Hunter, perhaps more than any other American artist of his day, introduced fresh and sophisticated European concepts into the American design vocabulary.

Note: The name "Dard" was passed on to two subsequent generations. In this book, "Dard" refers to Dard Hunter, the subject of this book; "Dard II" to his son; and "Dard III" to his grandson.

IO Two examples of Dard Hunter's iconic rose design. Left: Detail from the cover design of Dard's 1908 *Vulcanized Fibre* pamphlet (page 76). Right: Detail from back cover of *The Fra*, May 1908 issue (page 63).

NOTES

In these notes, the following abbreviation is used (see Selected Bibliography, page 110, for a full citation):
LWDH   Hunter, Dard II, *The Life Work of Dard Hunter*, vol. 1

1. Dr. Graham Dry to Lawrence Kreisman, e-mail correspondence, 14 January and 16 March 2011.
2. Dard Hunter II referred to his father as "the master of master craftsmen in other mediums." LWDH, 1.
3. LWDH, 1.
4. LWDH, 1.

PHIL HVNTER

A yovng conjvrer who keepſ ovt oƒ the trod den pathſ ✻ ✻ ✻

DARD HVNTER

■ Dard's first title page, designed in 1902 for a brochure illustrating the magic performances by his brother, Philip Courtney Hunter. A border accented with stylized stems and red buds frames the title. The artist signed his name at the bottom.

The Artistic Bent Emerges

WE SOMETIMES SAY that someone is a "natural," born with certain gifts assured through genetics. In the case of William Joseph "Dard" Hunter (1883–1966), perhaps there is some truth to this idea.

His father, William Henry Hunter (1852–1906), was owner and editor of the Democratic newspaper the *Daily Gazette* in Steubenville, Ohio. William Henry was weaned on the four-page *Sentinel*, a weekly newspaper in Cadiz, Ohio, in which his own father, Joseph Hunter (1804–1886), had invested and which William Henry helped produce. Joseph Hunter also had a cabinet shop and a small brass foundry and produced mahogany furniture and an array of useful items such as brass door knockers and andirons.[1]

Along with being a newspaper owner and publisher, William Henry Hunter was an amateur woodcarver; he may have honed those skills under his father's tutelage. He also learned how to make ceramics with a Steubenville friend, William A. Long. In 1879 they had visited the Cincinnati Industrial Exposition and seen firsthand the work of accomplished woodcarvers, as well as the wares being produced by Rookwood Pottery. After years of experimentation with glazes and firing, in 1891 Long, Hunter, and Alfred Day of the Steubenville Pottery Company combined letters from the beginnings of their last names to form the Lonhuda Art Pottery Company.[2]

William Joseph "Dard" Hunter was born in Steubenville, Ohio, in 1883. The nickname may have been attached to him when his older brother, Philip, mispronounced the word "darling," the affectionate term for the new baby. Dard grew up at a time when America was shifting from an agrarian society to an urban and industrial one. While Dard's father was an ardent proponent of modern advances such as the automobile, he was equally concerned that handcrafts not be sacrificed in the name of progress.[3]

Dard turned to graphic arts at an early age, having been exposed to them in Steubenville, where he grew up around printing house presses, stone slabs, and type cases. In addition to watching the presses roll out the daily and weekly newspapers, he observed the production of printed promotional flyers (for circuses, fairs, and traveling theatrical companies), which employed huge wooden type in red ink on yellow poster paper. Dard recalled that at the age of eight or ten, he was instructed in typesetting by Mr. Feckey, the foreman of the *Daily Gazette*.[4]

Dard had vivid memories of his family's visit to the World's Columbian Exposition in Chicago in 1893. The visit was prompted by the exhibition of several pieces of Lonhuda pottery and several examples of his father's wood carving. After exposure to the great variety of crafts on display, his father, William Henry, was inspired to prepare a column advocating the teaching of drawing and manual training, an approach to teaching that recognized that some children were less successful at traditional methods of learning language and math skills but could excel when their energies were applied to handwork. Dard claimed that this article, reprinted in *The Times* of London, influenced the establishment of drawing in the curricula of some English schools and later its introduction into many American public schools.[5] As a consequence, Dard's father would have been supportive of Dard's vocational pursuits.

Dard continued to experiment with graphic arts in Chillicothe, Ohio, where the family moved in 1900 after his father sold the Steubenville paper and joined his brother George as copublisher of the *Advertiser*. They combined it with other Chillicothe papers, the *Daily News* and the *Ross County Register*, to form the *News-Advertiser*.[6] Dard was asked to draw portraits, buildings, cartoons, and ephemera in the "chalk-plate" process. This was a method of preparing a steel plate by coating it with chalk and liquid gelatin, cutting away the design, and pouring heated metal onto the plate to create a mold from which the printing was done.

During 1901 and 1902, Dard and his brother used the *News-Advertiser* offices to produce a pamphlet that described and illustrated Philip's magic acts. They called their private venture the Yoctangee Press ("Yoctangee" is a Native American word for paint or pigment).

11 Display of Lonhuda Art Pottery at the Chicago World's Fair, 1893.

This pamphlet, which was Dard's first effort at color printing and included his first title page (page 14), prefigures his early work at Roycroft in the handmade type style he chose to use and the tulip and leaf embellishments he drew. During his pre-Roycroft days, Dard had been exposed to contemporary graphic design ideas that moved away from realistic depiction of objects and nature toward flat, stylized, or conventionalized interpretations that set off and harmonized with, but did not overwhelm, the written piece.

The old-style lettering might have been something he observed in reading *The Philistine*, to which his brother subscribed. His father disliked Philip's literary choice. He viewed Elbert Hubbard as a hypocrite for chastising the ostentation of wealthy people while, at the same time, using his eccentric and idiosyncratic dress, long hair, oratory talents, and advertising prowess to draw attention to himself. "Certainly there is no excuse for a man being a miser, whether it be of talent or money; if he have either one, it is his duty to give the benefit, but it is expected that there shall be a fair exchange."[7]

12 Above: Dard's cover for "Ohio History Notes and Comments," a piece written by his father, published May 20, 1903. Dard's graphic experiments combine some words with all capital letters and others with uppercase and lowercase letters. He drew a realistic seal of the state of Ohio, a building (probably the first state capitol) and the leaf and flowers of the buckeye, which earned a place as the official state tree. A variant of the swallowtail-shaped Ohio state flag, adopted in 1902, was used in a repeat pattern at bottom left and top right of the cover.*

* Hunter, Dard II. *The Life Work of Dard Hunter.* Vol. 1, p. 10.

13 Right: Hubbard's periodical *The Philistine* was nationally distributed. Philip Hunter was a subscriber, and Dard would have learned about Elbert Hubbard and his Roycroft community by perusing its pages. Image courtesy Dodge/Kreisman Collection.

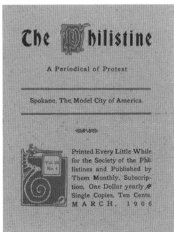

Dard's brother, Philip, was developing a name for himself as "Phil Hunter, The Wizard," performing magic acts regionally and eventually nationally. Dard joined him, doing a segment entitled "A Few Minutes in an Artist's Studio with Dard Hunter," during which he entertained audiences with chalk talks using colored chalk on tinted paper.[8]

In 1903 travels with his brother's troupe brought him to Riverside, California, where he stayed at the New Glenwood Hotel (later renamed The Mission Inn), one of the earliest hotels fashioned in the Spanish Mission style. This exposure to the Mission style in art and design made a lasting impression on him. He wrote to his brother, who had remained in Chillicothe because of illness:

> This hotel is positively the finest thing I ever saw. It is exactly as I would have made it. You can't imagine how it makes me feel to look at it. It almost drives me crazy. It is "Old Mission" until you can't rest. I have gotten more ideas in this one building than I have gotten from anything I ever saw. It is great. Positively grand.[9]

14 Left: A page from *Phil Hunter, The Wizard* (Cincinnati, 1903) showcases his younger brother's talents: "Dard Hunter the Artist In Art of Colors."

15 Right: Dard Hunter presents one of his chalk talks during intermission, drawing a life-size cowboy.*

* Hunter, Dard II. *The Life Work of Dard Hunter.* Vol. 1, p. 4.

16   The New Glenwood Hotel Dard saw in 1903 was a popular destination for snowbirds during the winter months. Above: The tearoom in the old Adobe showcased in this c. 1910 postcard was furnished with hammered lighting fixtures and Mission tables and rockers. Below: By 1908 the owners had planned a major expansion, shown in this c. 1920 postcard. Images courtesy Robert Rust (above); Glenn Mason (below).

Surrounded by beam ceilings, forged and hammered hardware, and a wide variety of furnishings, Dard found his earlier spark of interest in Arts and Crafts furniture (dating from a visit with Philip to the Pan-American Exposition in Buffalo in 1901) ignited in earnest by this experience.

His interest also was fueled by virtual encounters with the mythic Elbert Hubbard. While he did not share the same stage with him, Dard would have been well aware of the man and his community during his touring with Philip to a number of Chautauqua locations during the summer months.[10] Chautauqua was an education movement popularized in the late nineteenth century, particularly in rural America. Summer camps provided lodging and assembly halls for community gatherings and for lectures on myriad topics in science, current events, art, and literature, as well as preaching, music, and other entertainment. Hubbard was a familiar face on the Chautauqua circuit and one of the most sought-after speakers.

Certainly, Dard's exposure to *The Philistine* also stimulated his interest in the Roycroft community. He wrote to Hubbard asking if he could find a place for him after he graduated from university. While Dard's father may have had some negative opinions of Hubbard, he

17 *The Friendship of Amis and Amile*, translated from the ancient French into English by William Morris and also printed by him at the Kelmscott Press, 1894. Image courtesy Dodge/ Kreisman Collection.

must also have had some respect for him, because both of them had been inspired in their passion for handpress work and printing by the same man—the British designer and social reformer William Morris (1834–1896). Morris was credited with the revival of the fine press movement, combining type, hand-printing, good paper, and exquisite binding.

Dard recalled that his father, who introduced him to the skills required to make furniture and carve wood, also introduced him to fine printing:

> At this juncture, father, also keenly interested in fine printing, purchased a book that had a pronounced influence upon me. This unusual volume, with richly decorated borders and initials, had been printed in England several years previously by William Morris, an artist and craftsman about whom I knew little. I became so fascinated by this book and by father's description of the Kelmscott Press that I was eager to visit England, where such books had been made. Father agreed that later I might go abroad, but said that first I should have more schooling. After quiet persuasion I consented to enter Ohio State University, provided that I could choose my own course of studies.[11]

At Ohio State University, Dard had the opportunity to examine additional books from the Kelmscott and Doves presses. His exposure to and familiarity with these works served him well in winning the respect of his mentor-to-be, Elbert Hubbard.

NOTES

In these notes, the following abbreviations are used (see Selected Bibliography, page 110, for full citations):

BHOL   Baker, Cathleen A., *By His Own Labor: The Biography of Dard Hunter*
DHAMH   Dard Hunter Archives at Mountain House
MLWP   Hunter, Dard, *My Life with Paper: An Autobiography*

1. MLWP, 4.
2. BHOL, 5. See also Cathleen A. Baker, "The Lonhuda Art Pottery at Steubenville," *Style: 1900*, vol. 12, no. 2 (Spring 1999), 53–57.
3. Dard Hunter background was prepared by Dard Hunter III for the website www.dardhunter.com.
4. MLWP, 8.
5. MLWP, 13.
6. BHOL, 10.
7. "Ostentatious Waste," *Chillicothe News-Advertiser*, June 1904, DHAMH, as quoted in BHOL, 20–21.
8. MLWP, 19.
9. Dard Hunter to Philip Hunter, 15 November 1904, DHAMH, as quoted in BHOL, 18.
10. MLWP, 28.
11. MLWP, 28.

■ Beginning in 1907 and for many years to come, Dard designed letterheads. At Roycroft, his familiar fonts, square borders, and green and orange-red colors formed the headings for the Roycrofters, the magazines published by Roycroft, and the personal and business correspondence of Elbert Hubbard, as well as Dard's own School of Handicraft.

3

Becoming a Roycrofter

DARD HUNTER CAME OF AGE at the same time significant design trends were influencing the leading creative forces behind the American Arts and Crafts movement. The design movements of the late nineteenth and early twentieth centuries—British Arts and Crafts, French and Belgian Art Nouveau, and German and Austrian Jugendstil and Secession—were revolutionary in their time. They questioned established public taste, developed principles for design excellence, and encouraged artists and craftspeople through journals and exhibitions.

Many scholars consider William Morris's teachings and production of furniture, textiles, stained glass, books, and decorative objects to have been the catalysts for change in the way designers thought about their products. He encouraged stylized flat designs inspired by nature. His furniture broke away from heavily carved Jacobean and revival pieces to solid, simple, and functional furnishings designed to be in harmony with interior space. Morris's designs entered the mainstream through the commercial successes of his own Morris and Company and by way of sales in a major department store, Liberty. Morris's books, tiles, wallpapers, and textile designs inspired generations of designers. Key among these were A. H. Mackmurdo (1851–1941), founder of The Century Guild, and C. R. Ashbee (1863–1942), founder of the Guild of Handicraft, as well as C. F. A. Voysey (1857–1941) and M. H. Baillie Scott (1865–1945), two of the period's foremost architect-designers. Their designs and instruction led to less pedigreed work produced by students of the many industrial arts schools that sprang up throughout Great Britain.

British design pioneers influenced American architects to seek out simpler, more functional forms and to develop ornament that was derived from nature relating to contemporary life and locale. They also inspired designers to think comprehensively—both inside and out—so that fabrics, wall coverings, carpets, woodwork, and furniture worked together in harmony. Bungalows and Craftsman homes in rapidly expanding cities were sanctuaries from an increasingly busy public world—places where families could gather around the hearth and the piano to share conversation and music. There were Morris chairs and Stickley or Roycroft settles, or their regional equivalents, and window seats on which to curl up with a favorite book borrowed from the expanding network of Carnegie libraries or ordered from a Roycroft catalog and delivered by the postman.

New ideas in European and British interior design were promoted in *120 Interiors in Colours Designed by Modern Architects*, edited by C. H. Baer. Published in Cleveland, Ohio, by J. H. Jansen (1912), this was an American imprint of a German publication by Hoffmann-Stuttgart. Some of the plates showcased radical departures from highly carved and haphazardly decorated late nineteenth-century interiors.

18 Above: A Viennese hall designed by Josef Hoffmann.

19 Left: A hall designed by Marcel Kammerer in Vienna.

Images courtesy Dodge/Kreisman Collection.

20 Above: *The Studio Magazine of Fine and Applied Arts*, first published in London in 1893, was one of the most influential art journals ever published, inspiring similar journals in Europe and America. This drawing room, designed and executed by Liberty Co., is illustrated in *The Studio Decorative Arts Yearbook* of 1907.

21 Below: Will Bradley did a series of colored interiors of a home, which were published in *Lady's Home Journal* during 1901–1902 and reprinted in the French *Documents d'architecture moderne*, in which this design appeared. Bradley's application of conventionalized roses and tree forms in fabric, wallpapers, and leaded glass was as influential in America as were Baillie Scott's and C. F. A. Voysey's designs in Britain.

Images courtesy Dodge/Kreisman Collection.

Gustav Stickley's Craftsman workshop and Elbert Hubbard's Roycroft community were leaders in promoting simpler, less decorative forms in their versions of Arts and Crafts buildings and furniture. The vernacular furnishings of the Spanish colonial missions, the straightforward joinery of wood construction, and the innate beauty of clear grain fir, pine, and quartersawn white oak strongly influenced them. Both companies hired designers whose interest in and admiration for the work of British and Continental contemporary design had visible effects upon the works produced in these workshops. For Stickley, it was the beautiful inlaid furniture of Harvey Ellis; for Roycroft, it was the typography and the decoration of books, metalwork, and stained glass that came from the hand of the imaginative Dard Hunter.

The Roycroft community that Dard moved to in the summer of 1904 was a beehive of creative activity, with hundreds of skilled and unskilled workers tackling myriad projects in shops set up for printing, binding, furniture construction, and the creation of beautiful and utilitarian objects in hammered metal and tooled leather.

Immigrant workers sometimes brought with them ideas and design inspirations from their homelands. German artisans then working in the Roycroft shops may have provided the knowledge base that jump-started Dard's interest in Jugendstil and Secession motifs.

22 Arts and Crafts designers distanced themselves from high-style historicism to create quiet backdrops for family life with a few selected ornamental highlights, as in this suggestion for an entrance hall and living room by Harvey Ellis, illustrated in *The Craftsman*, August 1903 and October 1905. Image courtesy Dodge/Kreisman Collection.

For example, Louis Kinder had apprenticed to a master bookbinder in Leipzig[1] before coming to America and settling into the Roycroft shops in 1896 to train unskilled workers. Frederick C. Kranz, trained in leather modeling in Germany, later joined Kinder's staff.[2] Once fired up, Dard set himself on a course of study, experimentation, and, eventually, excellence in developing beautiful and progressive designs for Roycroft shops.

Hubbard's travels in Europe brought him closer to the work of designers he idolized, such as William Morris. Hubbard claimed to have met Morris on a trip to England in 1894, although no proof of this exists. Nevertheless, he did bring Morris's Kelmscott Press book designs into the Roycroft Press, and they continued to influence its designs until Dard's appearance.

Hubbard developed a following for his books. In addition to limited editions printed on special paper known as Japan vellum—with suede, three-quarter, or full leather bindings, and with added color, hand-decorated initials, and illuminations—he marketed a range of inexpensive options for readers.[3]

After some less than successful starts, Roycroft began to produce handsome and well-conceived book designs under the artistic direction of William Wallace Denslow and Samuel Warner.[4] Under Warner, title page designs for *Maud* (1900), *Poems by Edgar Allan Poe* (1901), and Jerome Connor's *Dreams* (1901) reflected the stylized floral borders popularized by William Morris's Kelmscott Press and other British presses of the time.[5]

Dard took advantage of the sophistication of Hubbard's printing enterprise to exploit color printing in titles, initials, borders, and colophons that drew upon British, Scottish, German, and Austrian design elements to shape a distinctive Roycroft look.[6] Hubbard would have appreciated and encouraged looking across the Atlantic for ideas. He claimed to have visited Darmstadt, outside Frankfurt, where he was impressed by the extraordinary art colony established in 1899 by Grand Duke Ernst Ludwig of Hesse.[7] It comprised housing designed by founders Josef Maria Olbrich, Peter Behrens, Hans Christiansen, and others, as well as a studio building providing space for their work.

He also claimed to have visited C. R. Ashbee's Guild of Handicraft, established in 1888 and moved to Chipping Campden, England, in 1902 so that workers could live and work together to learn crafts and life skills.[8] It was no coincidence that the enterprise in East Aurora bore similarities to these model artist communities. While Hubbard's Roycroft was organized as a business enterprise, there was no denying a socialist, utopian underpinning to the operation of his community, something that attracted Dard Hunter to it.

In the summer of 1904 the United States focused its attention on the Louisiana Purchase Exposition—the St. Louis World's Fair. It was an opportunity to see firsthand the accomplishments of American industry and art and to experience the most exciting designs coming

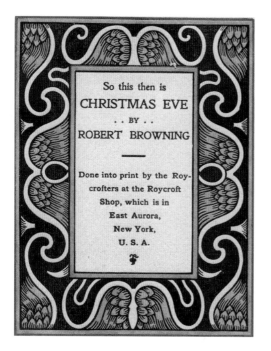

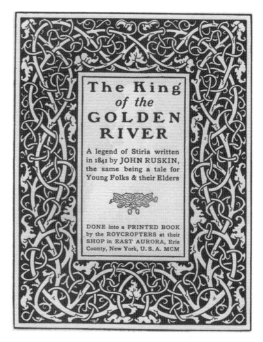

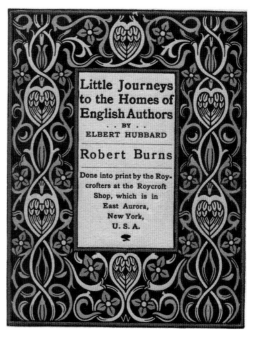

23 Works produced by Samuel Warner at Roycroft show the influence of William Morris's Kelmscott Press as well as the work of American designers making their own distinct contributions to book, magazine, poster, and advertising design. Clockwise from top left: *Christmas Eve* by Robert Browning, 1899; *The King of the Golden River* by John Ruskin, title page and initials designed by Samuel Warner, 1900; *Little Journeys to the Homes of English Authors: Robert Burns*, titles and initials by Samuel Warner, 1900; *Will o' the Mill* by Master Robert Louis Stevenson, portrait, ornament, and initials by Samuel Warner, typography by Andrew Andrews, 1901. Images courtesy Dodge/Kreisman Collection.

out of other countries. Germany and Austria both had a presence at the fair. Peter Behrens designed the catalog shown at the pavilions. In June 1904 Hubbard visited the fair and was impressed by the breadth of products demonstrating the progress of America, but also by the many foreign exhibits.[9] At the close of the fair, Hubbard's colleague and client John Wanamaker purchased the German display of interior architecture—comprising various rooms, fittings, and furniture—and installed it in his Philadelphia store, where it continued to gain public exposure.[10]

Dard missed this rare opportunity to see the German and Austrian designs that would later capture his imagination. Instead, he was determined to attend Roycroft even after having written to Hubbard and being told by him that there were no openings. He made the trip to East Aurora, New York, in July. This proved to be a wise move. He was quickly taken in by the Roycrofters and became a valuable contributor, eager to explore as many disciplines as possible. During his summer there, he would have his pick of media in which to experiment—drawing, ceramics, furniture making, printing, bookbinding, leatherwork, and metal.

24 Rendering of the courtyard of the German Pavilion for the 1904 St. Louis World's Fair by Josef Maria Olbrich, from *Architektur Olbrich*, Verlag E. Wasmuth, Berlin. Hubbard would have been won over by the architecture, exhibits, and objects brought over from Germany and Austria. Image courtesy Dodge/Kreisman Collection.

The ideal that attracted Dard to Roycroft and led him to remain there for six years was the concept of a utopian society where he could work uninterrupted without the pressure of earning a living. His motivation was to create beautiful objects and master the various crafts needed to do so. In his book *As Bees in Honey Drown*, Charles Hamilton commented, "Dard Hunter was the only Roycrofter who allowed his paychecks to pile up for weeks on end." This did not mean that he had other sources of income, but rather that he did not care about making money. His basic needs—food, shelter, exercise, and daily lectures that stimulated the mind—were provided for by Hubbard. This established the perfect atmosphere for optimizing creative output.[11]

25 Left: Dard Hunter's 1904 Mission chair, made of oak and mahogany, paint, red leather, and iron tacks, carries the welcoming message "Sit down & rest thy weary bones" on the back slat.

26 Right: Letter holder and a bookend by Dard, one of a pair, 1908–1909, hammered and repoussé copper.

27 Top: Starting construction of the Roycroft furniture shop, c. 1906. Dard is third from left; Sandy, Elbert Hubbard's son, is second from right.

28 Middle and left: Dard Hunter and fellow Roycrofters photographed c. 1906 during leisure hours.

When the expertise was not available on the campus, as was the case with stained glass, Hubbard arranged to send Dard to J & R Lamb Studios in New York City to learn the craft, which led to a series of stained glass windows for the Roycroft Inn. At the same time as Dard undertook the stained glass work, he completed his first design for the Roycroft Press—the title page of Hubbard's second edition of *The Man of Sorrows* (figure 31).[12]

Dard had access to current design trends in Europe through books and periodicals in the extensive Roycroft library. Hubbard subscribed to *International Studio* (the American reprinting of the British design monthly), *Dekorative Kunst, Deutsche Kunst und Dekoration,* and *Dekorative Vorbilder.* The first of these offered informative articles and reviews of exhibitions throughout Britain and Europe, as well as a short front supplement that kept readers abreast of the latest art and design events and talents in American cities coast to coast. The German publications showcased new commercial, institutional, religious, and residential architecture; interior design; decorative and fine arts; and book arts and typography, as well as exhibitions at the many museums, societies, and guilds throughout Europe. Exposure to the flat shapes, geometric patterning, and sans serif typefaces that characterized Secession design made an indelible impression on the young designer.

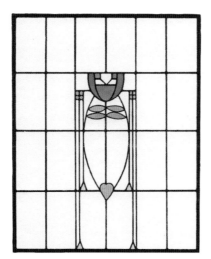 

29 Left: This stained glass design, inspired by Glasgow and German abstraction and conventionalization, became the basis for the reception room window in the Roycroft Inn, 1907. See other examples of Dard Hunter's glass designs on pages 96–103.

30 Right: Stained glass window for Kaim-Saal concert hall in Munich designed by Karl Ule, printed in *Deutsche Kunst und Dekoration,* vol. 1 (October 1897–March 1898), 41. Leaded glass such as this may have interested Dard in creating the clear leaded glass patterns he used in the Roycroft Inn. Image courtesy Dodge/Kreisman Collection.

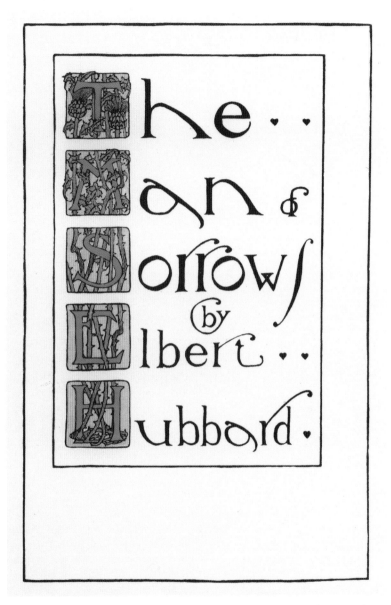

31 The first work Dard designed at Roycroft, in August 1904, was the title page to *The Man of Sorrows* by Elbert Hubbard. He continued to use the lowercase lettering developed here until he shifted away from his graphic design career in 1911. His later work in typography was patterned after Dürer. The red initials are intertwined with prickly green stems culminating in purple thistle blossoms. The thistle was one of the most popular flowers used by British Arts and Crafts designers, as it lent itself easily to conventionalized treatments. Hearts also were widely used, particularly as cutouts in British furniture and metalwork.

A drawback of German publications was, of course, that they were published in German. Notwithstanding, all of these volumes were heavily illustrated with black-and-white photographs, drawings, architectural renderings, and color plates depicting fine art, applied arts, bookbinding, and printing, as well as pattern and ornament from cities throughout Germany and Austria. There were occasional articles on British, Scottish, French, and even American designers. The numerous photo spreads of exhibitions and art fairs transcended national boundaries. German royalty and merchants commissioned British talents—M. H. Baillie Scott, C. R. Ashbee, and Charles Rennie Mackintosh—to design furniture and metalwork. These journals were extraordinary teaching tools.

Dard later reflected on his exposure to these works:

> Through these publications I became interested in "modern" tendency in design. These magazines were a monthly inspiration, and many of the commercial designs I made during my early years at the shop show this influence. Through a study of the German and Austrian art publications, I developed a strong desire to go to Vienna, where most of the secession movement had its origin. I wanted to study under the men whose work was shown in these publications.[13]

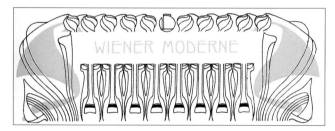

32 Above: Heading cover by Leopold Bauer in *Die Kunst*, vol. 4, no. 3, 89.

33 Left: German periodicals provided a wealth of interesting graphic designs that could be adapted by a creative and curious novice. Examples include work by Rudolf von Larisch of Vienna (top) and Alois Ludwig of Dusseldorf (bottom) illustrated in *Deutsche Kunst und Dekoration*, vol. 7 (October 1900–March 1901), 61.

Images courtesy Dodge/Kreisman Collection.

10. P. KERSTEN, ASCHAFFENBURG

28. PAUL BÜRCK, DARMSTADT

24. WALTER CASPARI, MÜNCHEN

19. TALWIN MORRIS, BOWLING (SCHOTTLAND)

NEUE BUCHEINBÄNDE

34 "Neue Bucheinbände" [New Bookbinding], *Dekorative Kunst*, vol. 4 (1900), 125. This page includes work by Paul Bürck, P. Kersten, and Walter Caspari in Germany and Talwin Morris in Scotland, showing how similar ideas were being expressed in multiple nations. Image courtesy Dodge/Kreisman Collection.

35 Edith Cornell, age about eighteen.

36 The Roycroft Printing Shop. Dard's studio was in the uppermost room of the square tower.

Fortunately for Dard, his plans fit those of Helen Edith Cornell, a New York City pianist and accompanist whom Hubbard hired for summer musicales at Roycroft. In March 1908 Dard and Edith married. Edith read and spoke German fluently and shared Dard's desire to go to Vienna, in her case to continue her musical studies with the well-respected teachers Marie Prentner and Dr. Theodor Leschetizky.[14]

If Dard Hunter had not arrived at Roycroft that summer of 1904, the Roycroft shops would have most likely continued on a path set initially by Hubbard. Books were designed as the poor man's William Morris, utilizing borders, initials, and illustration art in the Morris style. And there was nothing remarkably distinctive in the metalwork departments that would speak to modernity. There was no stained glass or jewelry making.

It was Dard's exploration of European modernism, stylized and conventionalized ornamentation, depiction of nature, and the incorporation of the simple square and spiral geometries in use in Secession design that led to Roycroft manufactures turning a corner and whetting the public's appetite. And despite Dard's departure in 1910, his designs continued to be used into the 1920s, because they were, indeed, some of the signature products of the Roycroft shops.

NOTES

In these notes, the following abbreviations are used (see Selected Bibliography, page 110, for full citations):

BHOL   Baker, Cathleen A., *By His Own Labor: The Biography of Dard Hunter*
HHH   Via, Maria, and Marjorie Searl, *Head, Heart and Hand: Elbert Hubbard and the Roycrofters*
MLWP   Hunter, Dard, *My Life with Paper: An Autobiography*

1. HHH, 97.
2. HHH, 97.
3. "The Roycroft Printing Shop," in HHH, 25.
4. HHH, 27.
5. HHH, 28–29.
6. HHH, 31.
7. HHH, 94.
8. While Dard II mentions these visits as fact, there is no documentation that Hubbard actually went to Chipping Campden, just as there is none regarding a meeting with William Morris. HHH, 94.
9. HHH, 94.
10. HHH, 94.
11. Dard Hunter III, e-mail correspondence with author, 4 May 2011. Also Charles Hamilton, *As Bees in Honey Drown: The Loves, Lives and Letters of The Roycroft's Alice and Elbert Hubbard*, SPS Publications, Tavares, Florida, 1997, 171. Hamilton bases his comments upon the earlier reflections of Felix Shay, who worked at Roycroft and wrote *Elbert Hubbard of East Aurora*, Wm. H. Wise & Co., New York, 1926, 152–154.
12. BHOL, 25–27.
13. MLWP, 43–44.
14. MLWP, 45.

■ While in Vienna, Dard designed this advertising cover for Colgate and Company at Elbert Hubbard's request. The bell-shaped flowers, yellow stylized flowers, and curvilinear leafed stems arise from the black-and-yellow planter box. These are all elements that Dard learned from his exposure to Viennese designers.

Secession Vienna

4

ARRIVING IN VIENNA in 1908, Dard and his new wife were enchanted by what certainly would have been a magical place after the rustic small-town streetscape of East Aurora. It was an imperial city resplendent with neoclassical and baroque palaces, churches, concert halls, and the Ringstrasse—a grand boulevard that had replaced the ancient city walls in the 1850s. As if swept along by Johann Strauss waltzes, residents and tourists flocked to restaurants serving the city's signature Wiener schnitzel, a breaded cutlet that sometimes extended past the boundaries of its plate, or Sacher torte, a decadent chocolate dessert originating at the Hotel Sacher.

The curvilinear patterns and stylized foliage and figures of French and Belgian Art Nouveau swept the world at the end of the nineteenth century, and central Europe had its own version, Jugendstil (literally, "youth style"). German and Austrian masters were brewing their own variation of the modern. Seceding from the Künstlerhaus, Austria's leading artist association, this group of artists combined the fluid lines of Art Nouveau with simple geometry and the controlled and limited use of surface embellishments and, ultimately, relied solely on form and materials to express the decorative in building and interiors.

Josef Hoffmann, Koloman Moser, Gustav Klimt, Otto Wagner, and Josef Maria Olbrich founded the Secession in 1897. Their exhibitions in a modern gallery designed by Olbrich that opened in 1898, not far from the Fine Arts Gallery, attracted attention outside of Austria. It became the place to be shown and discovered for designers from other countries. For example, Charles Rennie Mackintosh and C. R. Ashbee showed at Secession exhibitions, and their work received praise in newspapers and journals.

By the same token, the Vienna Workshop (Wiener Werkstätte), founded in 1903 under artistic directors Josef Hoffmann and Koloman Moser, produced a line of high-end products for the home that were displayed artistically in a Vienna showroom. The Werkstätte promoted an ideal of creating rooms that were total works of art in which all of the components worked in harmony—a concept known as Gesamtkunstwerk—and Werkstätte designers were fortunate to have a number of commissions in Vienna that allowed them to do just that. The pages of contemporary periodicals were filled with illustrations of remarkable buildings in which wallpapers, carpets, furniture, and lighting were the work of one designer or a team of designers. The Wiener Werkstätte opened a London showroom in 1906. Showrooms in Zurich, New York, and Berlin followed, with the group ultimately succumbing to financial problems in 1932.[1]

37 Wiener Werkstätte article, illustration by K. Breuer, for a garden pavilion, *Deutsche Kunst und Dekoration*, vol. 22 (April–September 1908), 75. The page borders and division of the page into type blocks and image blocks influenced the way in which Dard approached his page designs. Image courtesy Dodge/Kreisman Collection.

38 A simple overall repeat fills the ground of both the front and back of the cover of the *Catalog of the 10th Art Exhibition of the Austrian Secession*, Josef Hoffmann, 1902. Image courtesy Dodge/Kreisman Collection.

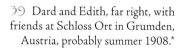

39 Dard and Edith, far right, with friends at Schloss Ort in Grumden, Austria, probably summer 1908.*

* Hunter, Dard II. *The Life Work of Dard Hunter*. Vol. 1, p. 146.

40 Above: *The Art-Revival in Austria*, The Studio Special Summer Number 1906, Offices of The Studio, London, Paris, New York, sported a title framed by tapering trees (possibly Italian cypress) rising from pots with square borders. This common modern motif was used by Dard Hunter in a number of his pieces (see pages 38, 82, 89, 97, and 98). Image courtesy Dodge/Kreisman Collection.

41 Left: Several Wiener Werkstätte postcards that Dard sent or brought home from his 1908 trip to Vienna formed the basis for the series of six cards printed for a promotional brochure on the Roycroft Inn in 1910 (see page 85).

42 For Vienna's railway network, the Stadtbahn, Otto Wagner built thirty-six stations and all the bridges. Two of these beautifully decorated pavilions, completed in 1898–1899, survive at Karlsplatz and have been restored. They were constructed using corrugated copper roofing and thin marble slabs hung upon an iron framework, a technique that Wagner would revisit in his post office. The results are pavilions that reveal their structure while providing a delightful ensemble of decorative embellishments in the green trim at the parapet and stylized gilt stencil work and trim.

43 Left: Joseph Maria Olbrich's Secession building (1897–1898) provided flexible exhibition space with the use of sliding walls. The simple cement stucco exterior of the cube is articulated with extended bays and façade treatments of built-up Jugendstil ornament including laurel leaf wreaths and scrollwork, some of it accented in gold. The laurel-leaf gilded bronze dome earned the building the not so affectionate nickname "The Golden Cabbage."

44 Right: Three gorgons over the entrance represent architecture, sculpture, and painting. The motto of the Secession— "Der Zeit ihre Kunst. Der Kunst ihre Freiheit." ["To the Age Its Art. To Art Its Freedom."]—welcomes visitors.

Images courtesy Wayne Dodge.

The Hunters would have seen some of these apartment buildings, rail stations, churches, post offices, and retail stores, as well as the Secession building itself. Highly evocative, they stood out from the traditional neoclassical and baroque architecture of their surroundings, showcasing the modernist advances sparked by this small group of progressive designers.

The letters Dard wrote to his mother expressed his excitement at finally being able to see firsthand buildings and designs he had seen only in pictures.

> Tomorrow we go to the "Wiener Werkstätte" and also this week to the model city [Sanatorium Purkersdorf] built by Otto Wagner who originated the modern art movement. There is a church there, the only one in the world built on modern lines [Kirche am Steinhof, also called the Church of Saint Leopold, 1904–1907]. Has windows by Kolo Moser which are the only ones in existence of Biblical figures drawn in the black style which is entirely modern. I have seen pictures of them in the German art magazines before I left the U.S. and thought them the greatest thing I ever saw.[2]

The following day, fresh from his visit to the Wiener Werkstätte, he wrote:

> I think its [sic] up to me to do from the U.S. what these fellows have done from Europe or Vienna rather as only Vienna is much influenced. It certainly shows advancement when the post-office [Wagner's Postsparkasse, 1904–1906] & public buildings are built by these fellows on modern art principles. The U.S. had better cut out its high buildings and get a little art into them . . . There are art exhibits everywhere and it is very strange to be in a place where there is some modern idea of things. Here an artist is not considered a half-witted fool as in many places in the United States. We can surely get some ideas from these fellows.[3]

While Dard was not able to enroll in a school during his stay in Vienna, he had some remarkable opportunities to meet and spend time with the leaders of its modern art movement. On May 21, he wrote:

> Went with Mr. Loos an architect for dinner and he afterwards took us to several of his buildings & rooms. He is modern in his style. Designed the Cafe Museum which was one of the first modern buildings here. He is quite good and a very nice chap. His wife was with us. His rooms are very good. He is not quite so extreme as Hoffmann but thinks he has the right idea. There is quite a bit of jealousy between these fellows. Also met Otto Wagner a man

45 Otto Wagner's centerpiece for the worship space of the Lower Austrian mental hospital at Steinhof (completed in 1907) differs from its predecessors in its use of thin marble slabs creating a bright, light-filled interior without interior columns. The stained glass windows were designed by Koloman Moser. The mosaic work in tile, marble, enamel, and glass was designed by Remigius Geyling and completed in 1913. The space was designed for the use of the "quieter" patients. Its pews provided ample space for supervisors to oversee the attendees. Image courtesy Wayne Dodge.

46 Windows designed by Koloman Moser and executed by Remigius Geyling were illustrated in *The Studio Yearbook of Decorative Art, 1909*, 61. Image courtesy Dodge/Kreisman Collection.

about seventy who is the founder of the modern school of design and teacher of Hoffmann & Moser also [Robert] Orley. Met Hoffmann also. Neither Hoffmann or Wagner speak English but Loos does. Had quite a fine time as these fellows are very celebrated being the leading modern designers in the world. Did not get to see Kolo Moser as he has just married a rich woman and does not go out much yet. Are going again to-morrow to Hoffmann & Moser's shop where we will be taken through. Were there the other day but could not go around it.[4]

Enthralled by Moser's stained glass windows at the Steinhof, on May 22 Dard went to Carl Geyling's stained glass shop, where they had been made. Dard designed a triptych for a Viennese restaurant window that incorporated the "black style" of Moser (see page 101). He used lead caming for lettering, which bears similarities to lettering used by Moser in the Steinhof windows and the poster for the *Secession XIII* in 1902.[5]

47 Stained and leaded windows with figures and lettering by Koloman Moser in the Kirche am Steinhof (also known as the Church of Saint Leopold). Images courtesy Cathleen A. Baker.

Dard II thought that his father attended the Kunstgewerbeschule, a fine art school of superior standing in Vienna; however, his father made no mention of it in his autobiography. He mentioned only his disappointment in being unable to enroll at the K. K. Graphische Lehr- und Versuchsanstalt Schule (Royal Imperial Graphic Teaching and Experimental Institute), operated in conjunction with the royal printing house of the Austrian government (see figure 54). He had been told that only students with diplomas from industrial schools were accepted, and there were no such schools in the United States at the time.[6]

There is no question that Dard absorbed Viennese design trends in the work that he did on his own during the five months he and Edith were in residency in Vienna.[7] In June and July 1908, through the auspices of his landlord's son, Fritz Hertz, he was introduced to the publishing firm of Hugo Heller und Sohn. He either brought with him from Roycroft or prepared in Vienna book cover designs to show Mr. Heller.[8] These designs were exceptionally accomplished and sophisticated, demonstrating his increasing understanding of Austrian typography and graphic imagery (see pages 88–89).

Dard was inspired by his tour through the Wiener Werkstätte facility and the range of products being produced there, and he had a great desire to enter a school of handwork. Upon his return from Vienna in 1909, he decided to risk starting a correspondence course for others that would provide students with the necessary tools to learn skills in various crafts—jewelry making, metalwork, and leaded art glass making. In April, *The Philistine* mentioned the course, and Dard produced a fourteen-page booklet he could send to prospective students of the Dard Hunter School of Handicraft (see pages 86, 108–109).[9]

In doing so, Dard took advantage of the public's increasing exposure to handcrafted goods and the increasing popularity of classes in manual arts in the public schools, as well as the fact that many new bungalow homes were being built in expanding cities that could benefit from beautiful and useful products, which, with proper training, even those who did not attend school could make.

In this booklet, he stated that art was for all. Through the training supplied by his school, Dard claimed, he had enabled hundreds of men and women to make in their own homes beautiful pieces of jewelry and stained glass windows similar to those he had made himself. "Things made by hand," he wrote, "are prized above everything and are constantly in demand, for the machine-made article no longer finds its way into the refined American home."[10]

He also claimed in an advertisement in the April 1909 issue of *The Philistine* to have worked in the leading art shops in Vienna, Munich, and Darmstadt.[11] This was an exaggeration of his experience in order to promote himself and his work. In fact, he had not found a position in

48   Peter Behrens's alphabet, which appeared in "Behrens Initialen" Originalerzeugnis Der Rudhard'schen Giesserei, Offenbach A. M., published in *Petzendorfer Schriftenatlas*, Verlag Julius Hoffmann, Stuttgart, Germany. It had a significant impact on Dard, and it appeared in several variations in his Roycroft work starting in 1907 (see pages 75 and 77).

Austrian and German publishing houses promoted modern design. The journal *Die Kunst unserer Heimat*, vol. 7 (1912), 31–42, carried examples of the work of The Ernst Ludwig Press, which showcased the designs of F. W. Kleukens (figures 49–51).

49 Top: Double title page from *Buch Esther* (Book of Esther). Richness of ornamental borders, stylized figures, and the use of gold ink to complement the black ink make for a stunning ensemble.

50 Middle and left: Initial letters become works of art in the hands of a creative graphic designer.

Images courtesy Dodge/Kreisman Collection.

51 *Daphnis und Chloe.* A less elaborate example of work by F. W. Kleukens has a tight ornamental border framing the title and an imaginative Pan with pipes filling the central vertical space. Image courtesy Dodge/ Kreisman Collection.

Vienna, and it was only while on the way home to the United States from Vienna that he and his wife briefly visited Darmstadt and Munich.

The jewelry designs illustrated in his booklet were definitely the kinds of pieces being produced in Pforzheim, the leading center of jewelry making, by Theodor Fahrner and others, as well as by artisans in Vienna, Munich, Darmstadt, Hamburg, and elsewhere. Dard's work was to be produced in sterling silver set with opaque semiprecious stones and occasionally enamel. Most combined abstract patterns—curved or straight-edged compositions—with vertical pendants or drops.

In his copper metalwork designs with fellow Roycrofter Karl Kipp, Dard achieved some of the finest American adaptations of Viennese Secession vocabulary. Their work

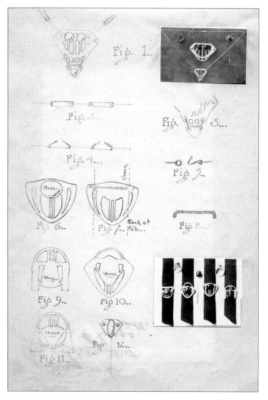 

52 Left: Last page of Dard's *Instructions for the Making of Hand-made Jewelry*, March 1909. Image courtesy Roycroft Arts Museum / Boice Lydell.

53 Right: Dard's stained glass and copper wall lantern, made for sale and shown in a 1910 Roycroft catalog, incorporated geometric glass, square cutouts, and tight spiral metal framing typical of Wiener Werkstätte motifs.

incorporated German silver squares on finely hand-hammered surfaces of vases, boxes, and desk accessories. They also crafted tightly curled tailpieces on hammered copper bases and lighting fixture frames.

During 1909 and 1910, Dard also expanded his printing repertoire to include letterheads, business cards, bookplates, and book designs. They incorporated Viennese-style lettering and motifs that differed from his earlier work, indicating his interest in seeking a fresh approach. He prepared a promotional brochure that included six cards showing the buildings on the Roycroft campus (see page 85). They were based directly on Wiener Werkstätte postcard designs, characterized by geometric borders; conventionalized figures, buildings, and landscapes; and deeply saturated contrasting colors (see figure 41).

Additional exposure to Viennese design and the possibility of studying at an accredited arts institution were obviously part of Dard's vision as he contemplated a second trip to Europe with his wife in the fall of 1910. In his autobiography, he described his creation of an elaborate diploma from an imaginary American industrial arts school, using parchment, gold seals, and silk ribbons to give it an air of authenticity that would impress Dr. Josef Maria Eder, the director of the printing school who had rejected his earlier application.[12] His strategy worked.

NOTES

In these notes, the following abbreviations are used (see Selected Bibliography, page 110, for full citations):

BHOL Baker, Cathleen A., *By His Own Labor: The Biography of Dard Hunter*
DHAMH Dard Hunter Archives at Mountain House
LWDH Hunter, Dard II, *The Life Work of Dard Hunter*, vol. 1
MLWP Hunter, Dard, *My Life with Paper: An Autobiography*

1. Kreisman, Lawrence, "Discovering Secession Vienna," *Style 1900*, vol. 23, no. 3 (Fall 2010), 69.
2. Dard Hunter (DH) to his mother, Harriet Browne Hunter (HBH), 17 May 1908, DHAMH, as quoted in BHOL, 38.
3. DH to HBH, 18 May 1908, DHAMH.
4. DH to HBH, 21 May 1908, DHAMH.
5. Cathleen Baker, "Sleuthing for Dard Hunter in Vienna," *Craftsman Homeowner*, vol. 6, no. 1 (Winter 1994), 11. See also BHOL.
6. MLWP, 46.
7. LWDH, 128.
8. While Dard II claims that four of his father's designs were published in 1909, Cathleen Baker was unable to verify this. "Sleuthing for Dard Hunter in Vienna," 12–13.
9. LWDH, 119. See Appendix 2 of this book.
10. LWDH, 23.
11. Advertisement, *The Philistine*, vol. 208, no. 5 (April 1909).
12. MLWP, 48.

■ Dard applied what he'd learned in Vienna to his book cover and title page for *Penrose's Pictorial Annual: The Process Year Book*, vol. 17 (1911–1912), edited by William Gamble, A. W. Penrose and Company Ltd., 109 Farrington Rd., London (Norfolk Studio). The title page above utilized a Secession leaf and bell flower border echoed in the central medallion by bell flowers and curvilinear embellishments. For this work, Dard placed his initials (DH) at bottom right.

Vienna, London & Home

5

IN 1910, DURING THEIR SECOND EXTENDED STAY in Vienna, Dard and Edith were joined by Sterling Lord, a friend who had apprenticed in bookbinding at Roycroft. This time Dard successfully enrolled in a design course at the K. K. Graphische Lehr- und Versuchsanstalt Schule.[1] According to his son, Dard was highly enthusiastic about his classes, especially in the department of graphic arts, where he studied lithography under Professor Viktor Mader, whom he thought was exceptionally fine. Another instructor, Professor Hubert Landa, taught drawing from nature, which was not exactly what Dard sought, given his already proficient abilities in stylized or conventionalized interpretation of nature. No English was spoken in the classes, and consequently he most benefited from courses in lettering and lithography, where lecture was less critical than seeing and doing. Dard boasted that Dr. Mader was so impressed with his skill that he wondered why he was even attending. By November he had dropped all classes but lithography and lettering. On receiving a diploma in February, he expressed reticence about accepting it, since he had not completed the entire course.[2]

54 C. O. Czeschka, K. K. Hof und Staats Druckerel, Wien [State Printing House], Vienna, *Deutsche Kunst und Dekoration*, vol. 22 (April–September 1908), 13. The K. K. Graphische Lehr- und Versuchsanstalt Schule, which Dard attended in 1910, was operated in conjunction with the State Printing House. Image courtesy Dodge/Kreisman Collection.

Nevertheless, his work showed that his skills—those he had learned on his own and those he had developed during his studies in Vienna—would be marketable elsewhere. The experience also made him aware of his maturity. He now had a desire to establish new paths and experiences; he had outgrown Roycroft. Dard reflected on returning to America:

> My mind, however, does not run East Aurora way as I believe I have fully recovered from the disease. Poetically speaking, I have been vaccinated by the virus of something better, something nearer the ideal. My time is spent, I believe, as my mind seldom reaches back to that beautiful little village with its surface of good cheer and its gizzard of strife, jealousy and hate.[3]

To find a paying position in a commercial art studio, the Hunters relocated to London in February 1911 after stopping in Dresden, Berlin, and Hamburg. Though they were not interested in living in a large city, there was appeal in contemplating a future location in the English countryside as steady income flowed in.[4]

Dard was initially hired by The Carlton Studio. After less than six weeks there, he went to the Norfolk Studio, run by American and British partners, and by April 10, 1911, he had started work. His letters home indicate a desire to be on his own—perhaps in the rare book trade or his own printing house—foreshadowing later accomplishments.

Some of the design work he did for Norfolk repeated his earlier work at Roycroft (dating from 1908). A promotional cover for *Green's Cigar Book* was almost identical to his *Vulcanized Fibre* cover, and the letterhead for the same firm simply repeated his charming title work with vine and grape leaves for *The Rubaiyat of Omar Khayyam*. There was little remarkable or innovative in the work of this period. His most creative and enthusiastic period behind him, he was simply making a living rather than following his passion.

He enrolled in an evening class at the Finsbury Technical College of London, established in 1883 as a model trade school for the training of artisans. Dard studied enameling and cloisonné under Alexander Fisher, one of the foremost Arts and Crafts metalworkers. He received a second place award for his cloisonné. For his prize, he selected Lewis F. Day's *Ornament and Its Application*, published by B. T. Batsford, London, in 1904—a most appropriate book for him.[5]

While visiting the Natural History Museum (now the Science Museum), Dard had the good fortune to observe a new exhibition that showed how handmade paper was made. The craft had ceased to exist in the United States after the L. L. Brown paper mill in Adams, Massachusetts, closed its doors in 1907. This was Dard's first opportunity to see firsthand how plant fibers were manipulated to form a sheet of paper. More importantly, the exhibition caused him to realize that a very critical trade had been lost to the industrial revolution in America; from that day forward he was dedicated to its revival. It was a "Eureka" moment for him.[6]

By November, Dard had closed the early chapters of his work life and returned to the United States. After a stay in Chillicothe, he and Edith settled into a country property near the village of Marlborough-on-Hudson, New York—not so different from the idyllic English countryside residence they had envisioned. Within a year, Dard had built a small mill and begun producing handmade paper utilizing the techniques gleaned in London. He soon had orders from every prominent etcher in America.

55 Above: Paper mill at Marlborough-on-Hudson, New York. Left: Dard (far right) and others in front of the paper mill, c. 1913.

56 The interior of the Hunters' cottage was quintessential Arts and Crafts. Mission oak rockers faced the hearth, along with a hall bench with true tenons and butterfly joints announcing its honesty of structure and materials.

While Dard had determined that there was a demand for handmade papers and income to support a commercial enterprise, maintaining such an endeavor had very little appeal for him. Instead, he began the arduous task of cutting the punches for and casting a new typeface, just as Johannes Gutenberg had done 450 years prior. It was his intent to master all aspects of bookmaking in order to create true harmony of paper, type, and printing. In 1916 he became the first person in the history of printing to single-handedly produce an entire book—*The Etching of Figures*—by the fifteenth-century hand method. For the next fifty years, his passion for the study of paper took him around the globe and led to his writing eighteen volumes on the subject of papermaking.

When he looked back on his early adventures and creative output in the graphic arts, he saw them as a diversion from the true work he was destined to do. Nevertheless, one century after their creation, Dard's beautiful combinations of text and graphics continue to delight and inspire designers, craftspeople, and homeowners.

NOTES

In these notes, the following abbreviation is used (see Selected Bibliography, page 110, for a full citation):
LWDH   Hunter, Dard II, *The Life Work of Dard Hunter*, vol. 1

1. LWDH, 142.
2. LWDH, 142.
3. LWDH, 142. There is no further elaboration of these sentiments to explain why his experiences at Roycroft, expressed so positively early on, had by this time left him with such a negative view of the community and its guiding light.
4. LWDH, 151.
5. LWDH, 153.
6. Dard Hunter III, e-mail correspondence with author, 4 May 2011.

~ THE ~
PLATES

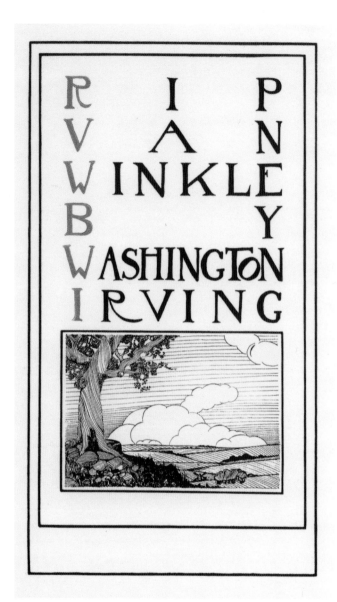

■ Dard's second book design, done in early 1905, was *Rip Van Winkle* by Washington Irving. The stylized illustration technique he used here is similar to that of Louis Rhead, a former Roycroft artist. The toned landscape scene on the cover is prelude to a series of scenic initials throughout the book. In the initial "H" (above), the stream in the foreground leads the eye toward the waterway, the windmill, and the distant horizon. Dard might have been testing out Arthur Wesley Dow's instructions to artists in his influential book, *Composition: A Series of Exercises in Art for the Use of Students and Teachers,* published in 1899 and widely available. In it, Dow encouraged artists to reinterpret nature with line, mass, and color rather than copying directly from it.

■ In 1905 Dard designed the double title page, decorative initials, and triangular tailpiece for Elbert Hubbard's *Love, Life & Work*. The leaf and stem border recalls those of William Morris's Kelmscott Press, only greatly simplified and less dense. Morris's press also utilized deep orange or red inks for key letters and words. Hubbard was pleased with this design, writing, "Dear Dard. Your double title page is great, the best ever."*

* Hunter, Dard II. *The Life Work of Dard Hunter*. Vol. 1, p. 24.

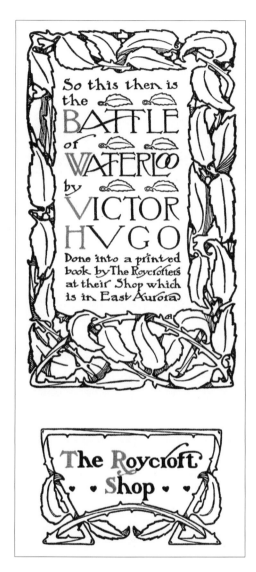

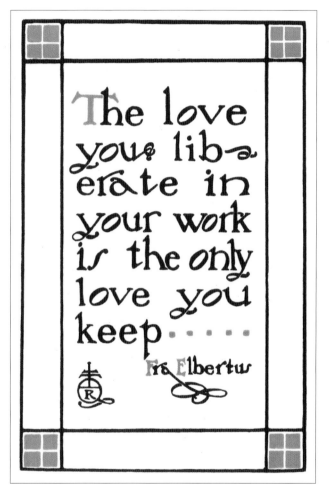

■ Left: Hubbard's satisfaction with Dard's *Love, Life & Work* art may have prompted the use of similar motifs in *The Battle of Waterloo* (1907).

■ Right: One of the most affordable and popular Roycroft products was the motto or epigram, such as the one shown here. Hubbard obviously enjoyed writing these concise comments on man's strengths and foibles. Dard probably created the German and Austrian motif borders and hand-lettered the mottoes. Some of his borders are almost identical to Peter Behrens's designs for Allgemeine Elektricitäts-Gesellschaft (AEG), the General Electricity Company in Germany.

■ The cover for *A Catalog of Some Books & Things* for 1905 and 1906 utilized four abstract tree designs. A common motif in British Arts and Crafts, it was also frequently used in German and Austrian design, sometimes as trees arising from planters. Dard used this motif in a number of works starting in 1908.

IMAGINATION IS SYMPATHY ILLUMINED BY LOVE AND BALLASTED BY BRAINS

■ By 1907 Dard had developed his emblematic "Dard rose," a stylized form that incorporates a "D" and an "H" as the center petals of a squared-off rose. He experimented with a number of approaches in *The Fra* and *The Philistine*. Dard II believed that Dard's inspiration came from a title page in the April 1905 issue of *Archiv Für Buchgewerbe*, a German bookbinding journal that was kept in the Roycroft library for the use of the artists. This decorated motto was written by Elbert Hubbard; it is from the back cover of the May 1908 issue of *The Fra*.

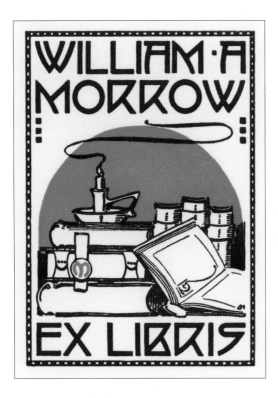

Artists were often called upon to design bookplates, and Dard was no exception. It was an opportunity to explore motifs, themes, and lettering that ordinarily might not have been used in book or poster work.

Clockwise from top left:

■ This bookplate for William A. Morrow was probably created in East Aurora, c. 1910. The square pendants below "Morrow" and the square beaded border derive from Dard's Vienna experience.

■ Eric Warne was an English acquaintance. This bookplate was probably designed in London in 1911. It displays the influence of Ralph Pearson, an artist friend.

■ Clara Ragna Johnson, a Roycroft photographer, later married Dard's cousin Junius K. Hunter. The poppy foreground at the bottom and the fairy-tale castle and cloud backdrop at the top frame the lettering, c. 1905.

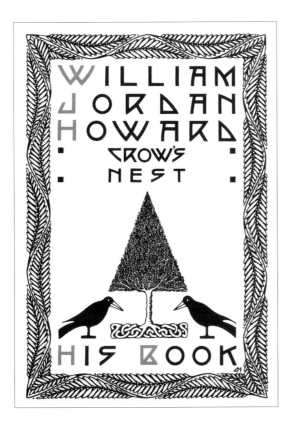

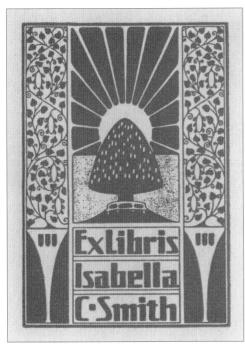

Clockwise from top left:

▪ This balanced and formal design for William Jordan Howard is bordered by modulated and stylized palm leaf forms and a triangular tree form. It most likely was created in East Aurora in 1908 and borrows from Viennese graphics of the period.

▪ Maurice Gaspard was at Roycroft and received Werkstätte cards from Dard (figure 41). The contrasts of foreground earth with its carpet of flowers, midrange rolling hillside and housing, and sunburst background make for a rich graphic. Probably drawn in Vienna in 1909.

▪ Isabella C. Smith's bookplate was probably drawn in Vienna on request of Elbert Hubbard, c. 1909.

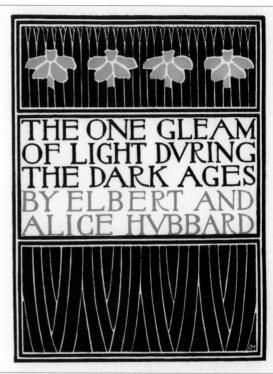

■ For Elbert and Alice Hubbard's dramatic 1906 play, *Justinian and Theodora*, Dard produced one of his most memorable title page spreads. It incorporates narcissus, whose black stalks below the title reappear above in a burst of orange blossoms. Dard designed initial letters, borders, and a colophon that incorporated the stalk and blossom elements to create a harmonious volume.

The design is similar to one by Paul Bürck (left), a Munich artist and a founding designer of the Darmstadt Art Colony, illustrated in *Deutsche Kunst und Dekoration*, vol. 4 (April–September 1899), 342. Image courtesy Periodical Collection, Seattle Public Library.

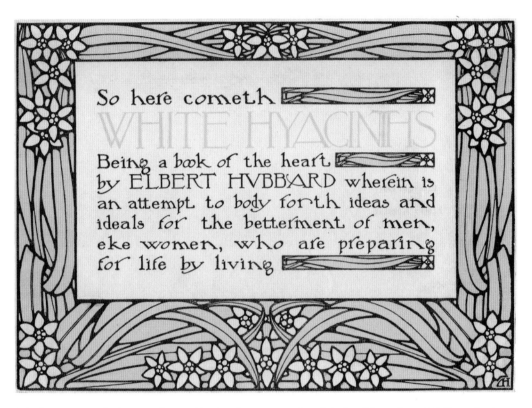

So here cometh WHITE HYACINTHS Being a book of the heart by ELBERT HVBBARD wherein is an attempt to body forth ideas and ideals for the betterment of men, eke women, who are preparing for life by living

■ While the majority of title pages designed by Dard were vertical, with *White Hyacinths* in 1907 he took advantage of the horizontal format with a border of intertwined and elongated leaves and contrasting white hyacinth blossoms strategically and symmetrically placed at center and corners. The design was popularized later in *The Tale of Two Tailors* (1909) and *Pig-Pen Pete* (1914).

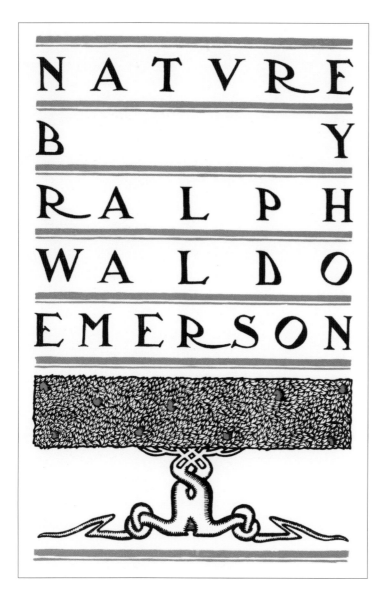

■ For *Nature* by Ralph Waldo Emerson, Dard created an abstract tree design in 1905. The central motif comprises knotted roots rising to a trunk that extends in curvilinear limbs to a topiary fruit tree, its horizontal mass supporting title and author lines above. The chapter endings are a reinterpretation of this motif in a triangle. The colophon is a variant of the twisted and knotted tree on the cover. The trunk is a solid vertical post, and the roots stretch out horizontally and rise vertically to embrace "The Roycroft Shop." Rows of red hearts complete the composition.

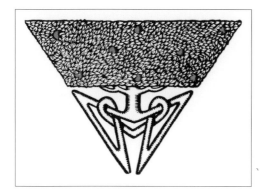

■ The red initial letters and scenic vignettes in *Nature* are much more sophisticated than those Dard prepared for *Rip Van Winkle* and closer in kind to the landscape style of the title page of that work (pages 58–59). In format, they break out of the simple rectangle to wrap around the text. Each initial scene uses a different tree, such as poplar, pine, and oak, in a series of equally spaced verticals that balance the horizontality of the foreground shrubs, middle ground hills and valleys, and background clouds.

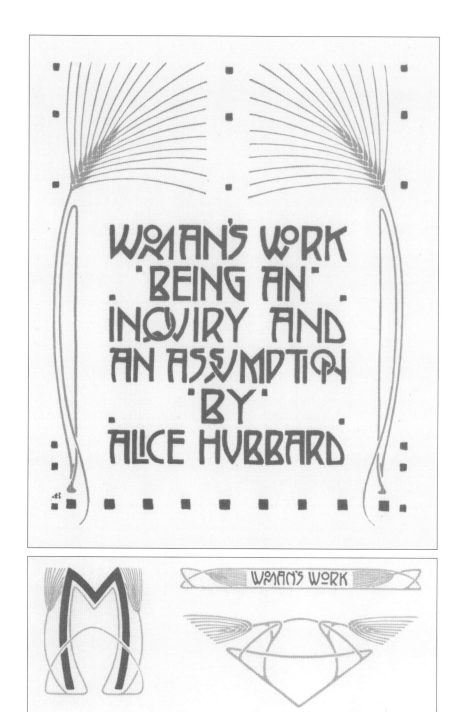

■ For Alice Hubbard's *Woman's Work*, published in 1908, Dard used delicate gold wheat sheaves to frame the substantial green letters on the title page as well as the initial "M," the page heading, and the chapter ending. He also used Viennese squares in two different sizes: the larger ones to ground the bottom of the page and the smaller ones to draw the eye to the base and the flowers of the wheat sheave frames. This design was repeated in *A Harvest Home Homily* by Elbert Hubbard in 1909.

■ Hubbard wrote an advertising brochure for longtime friend John Wanamaker. The title page for this 1907 piece uses flowerpots and conventionalized blossoms that Dard II claimed are almost identical to those pictured in the June 1905 issue of *Archiv Für Buchgewerbe*. Regardless of whether Dard had seen this specific issue, the motif was commonly used by British, Austrian, and German designers. It was featured in *The Art-Revival in Austria*, The Studio Special Summer Number 1906 (see figure 40).

A CATALOG OF BOOKS AND THINGS CRAFTY MADE BY THE ROYCROFTERS IN AN IDLE HOVR

1907 1908

■ The 1907–1908 Roycroft catalog used a symmetrical stem, leaf, and fruit border design. It appeared in larger form in Alice Hubbard's *The Basis of Marriage* in 1910.

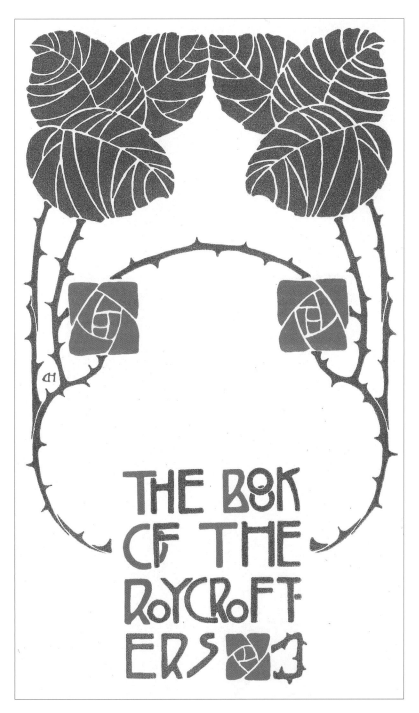

■ A similar symmetrical treatment of stylized roses, leaves, and thorny stems graces *The Book of the Roycrofters*, published in 1907.

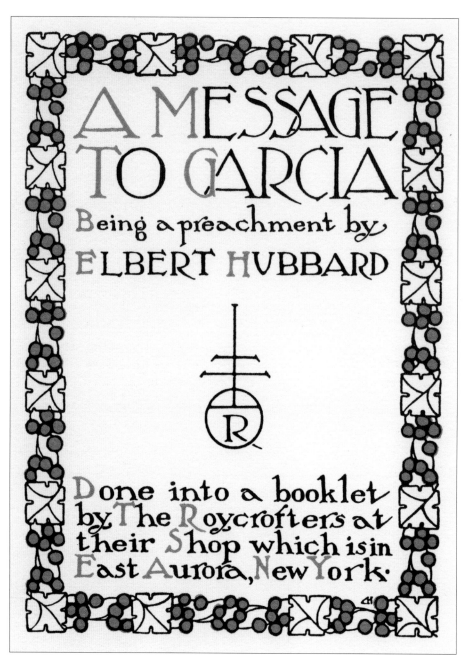

A MESSAGE TO GARCIA

Being a preachment by

ELBERT HVBBARD

Done into a booklet by The Roycrofters at their Shop which is in East Aurora, New York.

■ Elbert Hubbard's *A Message to Garcia*, initially published in the March 1899 issue of *The Philistine*, brought Hubbard a great deal of fame and led to numerous editions published by Roycroft that sold in the thousands. This special edition, published in 1907, has a title page border of squared leaves (a common motif of the British designers) and berries.

■ Twenty-five Viennese-fashioned initial letters with borders were first used in *The Philistine* beginning in December 1907. They show Dard's emerging interest in modern European design.

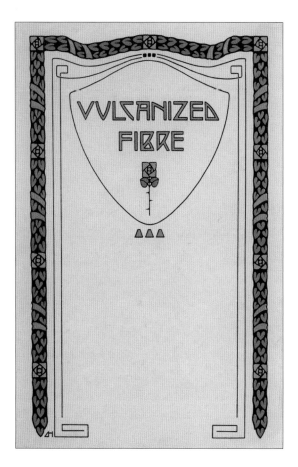

Clockwise from top left:

▪ The cover design of the 1908 *Vulcanized Fibre* pamphlet incorporates a garland border design similar to one Dard would have seen in the *Archiv Für Buchgewerbe* for 1906. The square rose is symmetrically placed within the border and is also the focus of the central graphic. Dard used this border in *Roycroft Leather Book* in 1909.

▪ Viennese-derived designs serve as the decorative treatment for this advertising cover, c. 1908. The red initials complement the tiny red square pendants and "eyes" of the curved triangles.

▪ The front cover design for the first issue of *The Fra*, April 1908, incorporates Dard's stylized orange-red rose with his thinly disguised initials—a central "H" framed by mirror image "D"s. The design was used until June 1915, a month after the deaths of Elbert and Alice Hubbard in the sinking of the *Lusitania*, when the cover was revised.

Clockwise from top left:

- The title page for volume 19 of Elbert Hubbard's 20-volume *The Complete Writings*, published by the Roycrofters between 1908 and 1915. The lettering is based on that found in the October 1906 issue of *Deutsche Kunst und Dekoration*.

- These initials were incorporated in *The Complete Writings*. They were influenced by the letters of Peter Behrens and similar designs in the October 1906 issue of *Deutsche Kunst und Dekoration*, and the backgrounds were influenced by designs from a March 1905 issue of *Archiv Für Buchgewerbe*.

- A set of initial letters was modeled on "Behrens Initialen" Originalerzeugnis Der Rudhard'schen Giesserei, Offenbach A. M. (figure 48), published in *Petzendorfer Schriftenatlas*, Verlag Julius Hoffmann, Stuttgart, Germany.

■ An engaging holly leaf and berry border for the back cover of *The Fra*, December 1908 issue.

■ The cover and title page squared leaf and grape designs of the Roycroft *Rubaiyat of Omar Khayyam*, published in the fall of 1908. *The Rubaiyat* was one of the most popularly published poems, coming out in virtually hundreds of common and limited editions with illustrations, photographs, and graphic treatments, including those by some of the most talented British and American designers and presses.

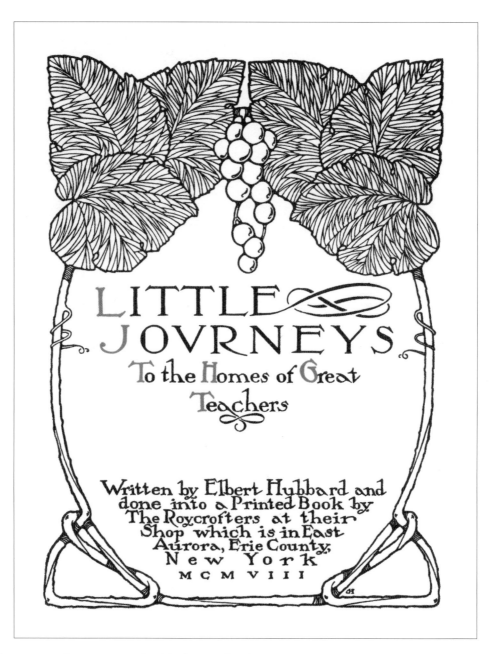

LITTLE
JOVRNEYS
To the Homes of Great
Teachers

Written by Elbert Hubbard and
done into a Printed Book by
The Roycrofters at their
Shop which is in East
Aurora, Erie County,
New York
MCMVIII

■ *Little Journeys* underwent a major face-lift when Dard took over. Conceived in 1893, the early series had a very traditional appearance. In 1908 it briefly shifted to a stem frame with grapes at the top (above). Shortly thereafter, it sported stylized yellow tulips and square green leaves framing Viennese-influenced lettering (opposite). The designs share much with the Midwestern Prairie School design of stained glass windows during this period. Dard would certainly have been exposed to this type of design, since Frank Lloyd Wright, William Gray Purcell, George Grant Elmslie, and others were regularly featured in the press. The Darwin Martin House, one of Wright's greatest domestic commissions, was completed in 1906 in nearby Buffalo.

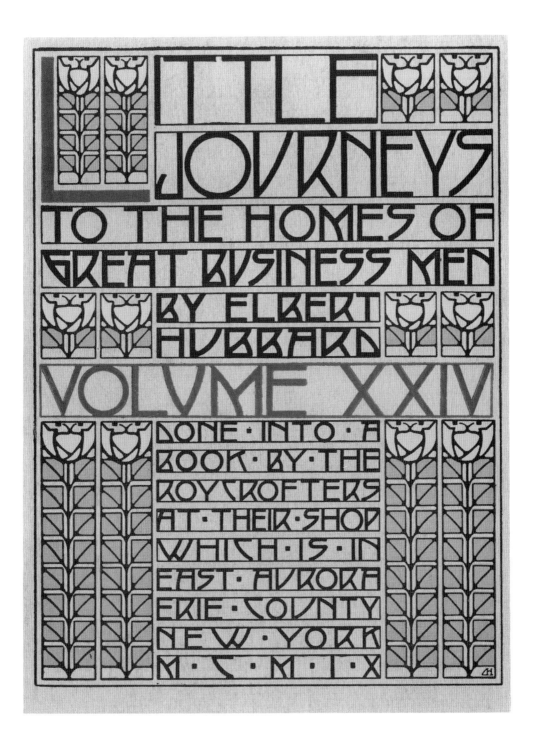

LITTLE JOURNEYS TO THE HOMES OF GREAT BUSINESS MEN BY ELBERT HUBBARD VOLUME XXIV DONE·INTO·A BOOK·BY·THE ROYCROFTERS AT·THEIR·SHOP WHICH·IS·IN EAST·AURORA ERIE·COUNTY NEW·YORK M·C·M·I·X

■ *Interior Decorations and Furnishings*, a 1906 sales brochure for Schwartz Eustis Co., Ltd., in New Orleans, incorporates a border of flower, leaf, and stem motifs, which also form the abstract square bush growing out of a flower box—the centerpiece of the composition. Dard II thought the design resembled "the delicacy of a fifteenth century illuminated manuscript but in a modern taste." In fact, it relates more directly to the overall pattern design of Otto Prutscher and other central European designers.

■ Left: Dard's 1909 design for Alice Hubbard's *Life Lessons* showed that he was inspired by contemporary patterns by German and Austrian designers. He used close-knit, spiraled leaf motifs stemming from a central point—a planter box—for the main image. All ornaments were tightly contained within geometric borders.

■ Right: The title page, chapter endings, and initials of *The Mintage*, published in 1910, are composed of bell-shaped and cartwheel-type flowers emerging from a ground of stylized leaves. The alphabet—all capitals—appears to have been one of Dard's favorites, judging from the number of times he used it between 1908 and 1910.

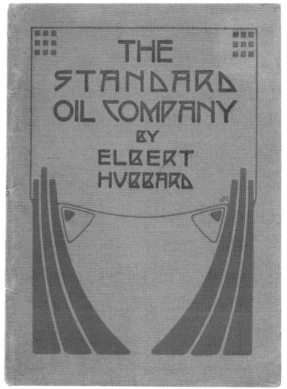

■ Left: In June 1910 Dard produced a beautiful Roycroft publication combining two written pieces, *Manhattan* by Joseph Clarke and *Henry Hudson* by Elbert Hubbard. The subject matter lent itself to circular medallions containing sailing ships. The use of green, red-orange, blue, and yellow make this one of his most colorful covers.

■ Right: The title page for a twenty-four-page booklet, *The Standard Oil Company*, by Elbert Hubbard (1910), has been interpreted as a subtle critique of the powerful oil trust. Its main feature is a conventionalized octopus with orange tentacles reaching out as if to grasp smaller companies, with blue-grey lettering suggestive of the color of oil.

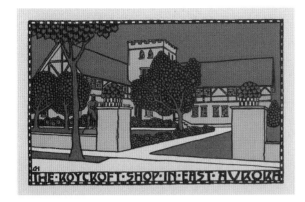

■ During his first stay in Vienna in 1908, Dard became acquainted with the production of colorful postcards by artists of the Wiener Werkstätte beginning in 1907. They were numbered in series to celebrate holidays, show off fashions, and illustrate the sights of Vienna. Dard sent them to family and friends (figure 41).*

These six five-color illustrations of the exterior and interior of the Roycroft chapel, shop, and inn definitely derive from that body of work, borrowing both the geometric frames and the saturated colors that popularized these cards.

* See *Postcards of the Wiener Werkstätte: A Catalogue Raisonné: Selections from The Leonard A. Lauder Collection*, edited by Elisabeth Schmuttermeier and Christian Witt-Dörring, Neue Galerie, New York, 2010.

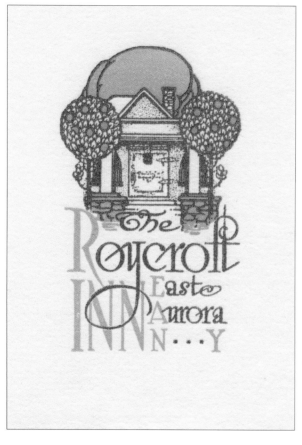

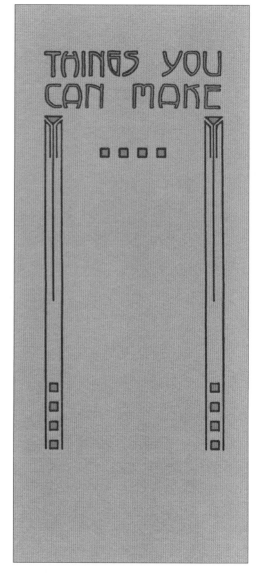

■ Dard's distinctive green and orange-red colors and topiary trees and bushes—reminiscent of the German and Austrian graphics he had been exposed to—promoted Roycroft enterprises. This letterhead design for the Roycroft Inn was created after 1907.

■ Right: Considering Dard's usual complexity of design and his ability to use color ink to great effect, it is surprising that the cover for this fourteen-page promotional booklet for the Dard Hunter School of Handicraft, entitled *Things You Can Make*, is so basic.

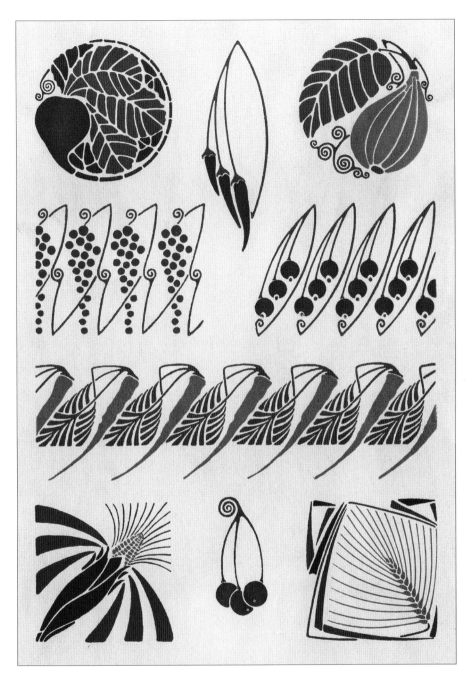

■ Conventionalized wheat, fruit, and vegetable designs. Dard II claimed these were created as a lithograph and were published in *Dekorative Vorbilder*, a house decorators' magazine issued in Stuttgart, Germany.

■ In 1908 Dard designed this title page for *Aus den Tagen des Knaben*, presumably to show the Viennese publisher, Hugo Heller und Sohn, what he could do with German-language titles. (The authorship was mistakenly credited to Gustave Flaubert; the correct author was Ernst Hardt.) From the black-and-white geometric patterned flower box emerges an imaginative rosebush, its descending branches culminating in roses that are repeated to fill out the lines with shorter words in the title.

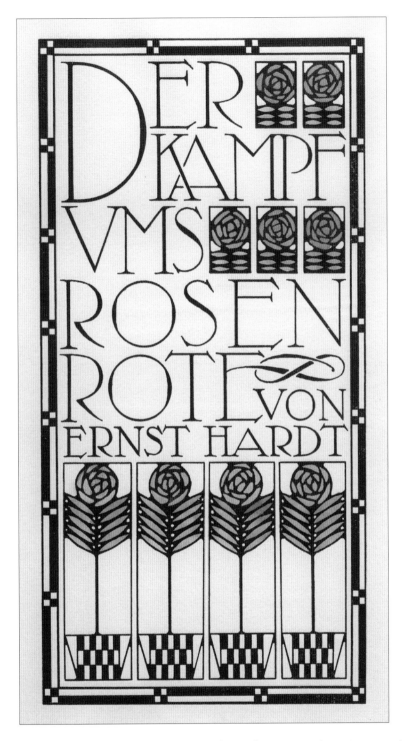

■ A more delicate letterform was used in the design of this title page for *Der Kampf Ums Rosenrote,* also by Ernst Hardt. It was likely created during Dard's first Vienna trip in 1908. He used a variation of his planter and a rhythmic series of upright roses.

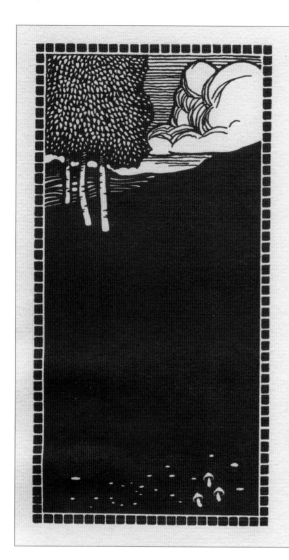

POETISCHE REISEN IN DEUTSCHEN LANDEN UND IM HEILIGEN RUSSLAND VON CARL LARSEN

■ Cover and initial letters for a book of poetry by Carl Larsen. Dard utilized the same stylized typeface as in *Aus den Tagen des Knaben* (page 88).

■ One of Dard's most accomplished Austrian designs was a 1909 double title page for *Im Land des Weins und der Gesänge und Im Schönen Portugal* by Carl Larsen. The lettering is Roman-inspired, and the design reflects his understanding of foreground (ground cover), middle (the stand of tapering tree trunks culminating in branches and leaves), and background (horizon and clouds) perspective. The pages are tied together by borders composed of squares of conventionalized ferns.

THE
PACIFIC PRINTER

WITH WHICH IS
INCORPORATED
THE PACIFIC
PUBLISHER

JANUARY, 1911
VOL. 5   NO. I

THE PACIFIC PUBLISHING COMPANY
SAN FRANCISCO, CALIFORNIA, U.S.A.

·DARD·HUNTER·· VIENNA·

■ Above: Dard's mastery of the elements of design that made Viennese modernism so dramatic culminated in this double title page created in 1908 for Oscar Wilde's *Salome*. It pictures Salome in profile, the tall robed figure on the left, holding up the severed head of John the Baptist. Dard's lettering breaks away from simple sans serif type with the addition of curling embellishments that are tied to the dress folds, the hair, and the beard on the facing page.

■ Opposite: Cover for *The Pacific Printer*, designed in Vienna in 1910 for the January 1911 issue for this San Francisco company. Bold sans serif lettering and the two large vertical, oval decorative plant motifs surrounded by an undulating border pleased the publisher, who remarked that it was "one of the handsomest, most striking and effective covers of any printing journal published."

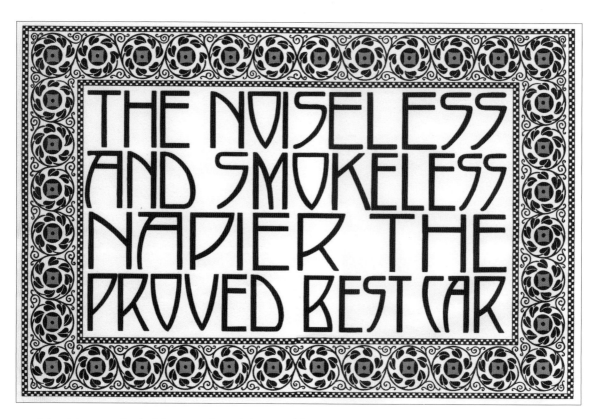

THE NOISELESS AND SMOKELESS NAPIER THE PROVED BEST CAR

■ Advertising cover for the Napier car, done while at Norfolk Studio.

■ This J. D. Siddeley motor carriage booklet cover, designed in 1911, may have been one of Dard's last commercial projects in England before returning home. While its design is crisp, colorful, and well balanced, it is not as memorable as some of his earlier designs.

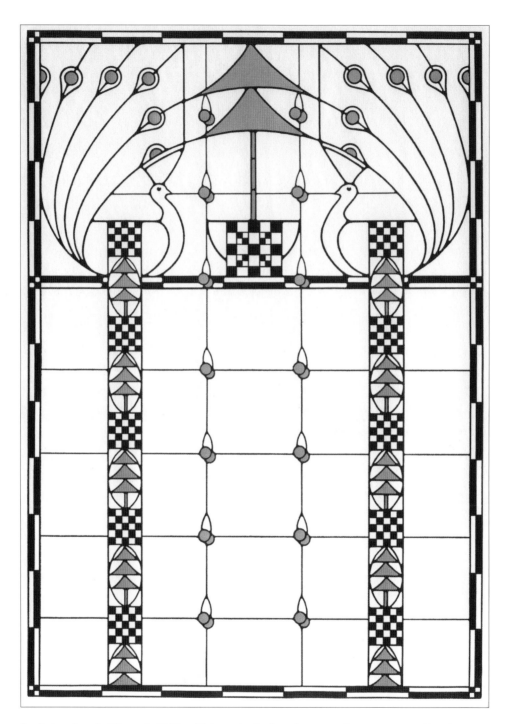

■ Peacock window done in Vienna in 1908, utilizing a checkerboard pattern, abstract trees, and berries.

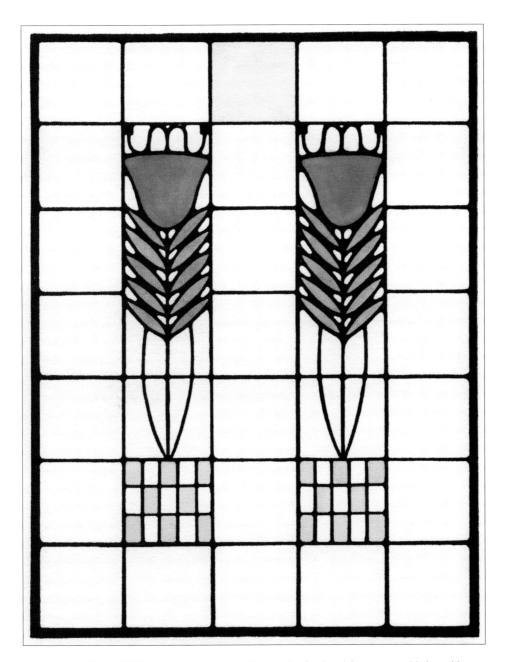

■ Revised design created in 1905 for a window incorporating a pair of stylized flowers, possibly lotus blossoms, with elliptical stems and angular green leaves rising from checkerboard planters—a Vienna motif that Dard used frequently. This window can be seen at the Roycroft Inn today (see page 4 for the original design).

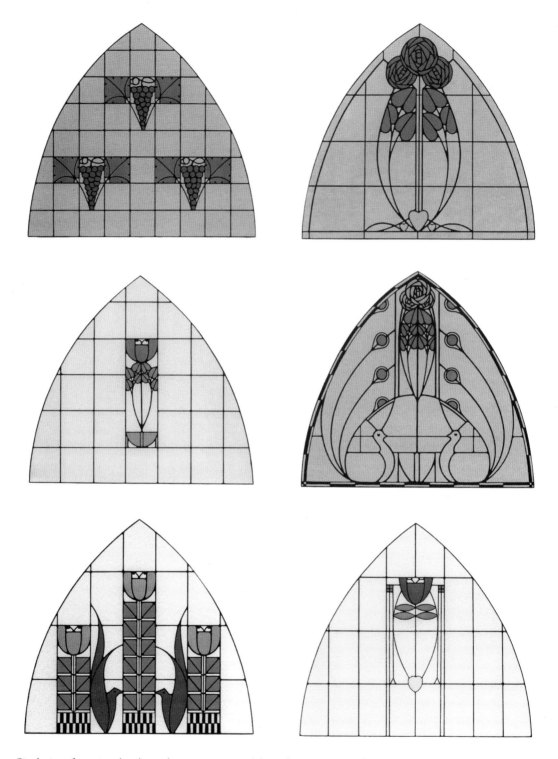

■ Six designs for pointed arch windows, 1904–1906. The only one executed (bottom right), made for the Roycroft Inn, had a conventionalized purple bud.

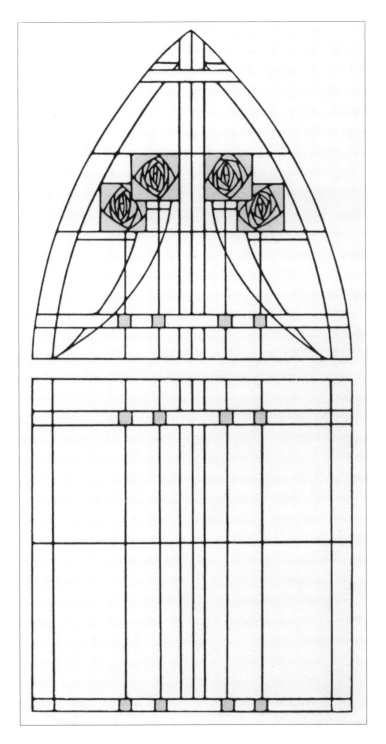

■ Rose window, c. 1905. The downward sweep of the rose stems counters the outward-pointed arch frame. By overlapping the squared roses, a slight three-dimensional effect is suggested.

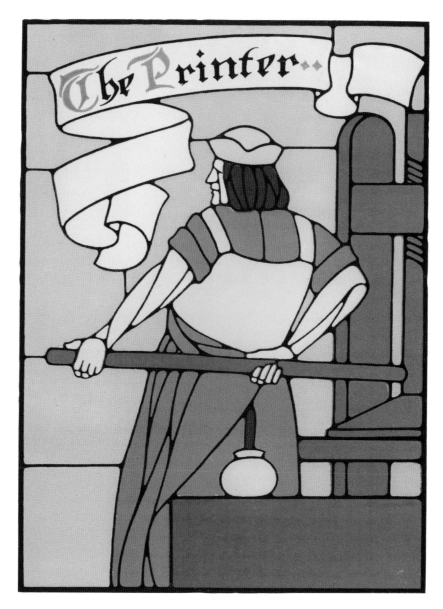

■ *The Printer*, one of three stained glass panels for a lantern at the Roycroft Inn. The other panels depict the architect and the sculptor. The frame of the lantern was made at the Roycroft copper shop by Karl Kipp, who embraced Austrian and German design motifs and incorporated their square geometries and curling embellishments into his work.

■ Designed in Vienna in 1908, this triptych for a stained glass window depicts servers bearing trays containing mugs of frothy beer, with elongated napkins draped over each arm. The mottoes read, from left to right, top to bottom: "He who drinks well, sleeps well; he who sleeps well, lives well," "Hops and malt, God bless them," and "He who doesn't love wine, women and song, remains a fool his life long." These designs were inspired by the Koloman Moser windows designed between 1898 and 1902 for the Kirche am Steinhof, also called the Church of Saint Leopold.

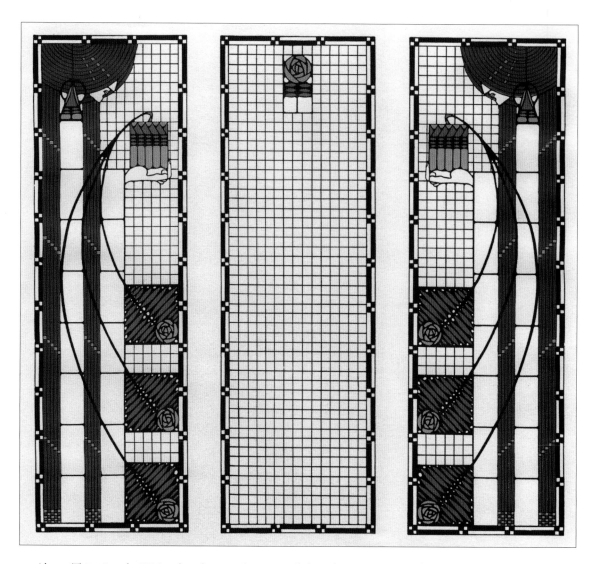

■ Above: This triptych, 1908, to have been made in stained glass, shows two women facing each other with their heads bowed in lamentation, holding urns of drooping green-leafed roses. The simple central panel is adorned with one upright red rose, symbolic of love.

■ Opposite: This drawing for a glass mosaic panel created in 1908 is extraordinarily complex. The rhythmic flow of spiraled green leaves contrasts with the more precise and severe pattern of squared red roses positioned at regular intervals in the long vertical hair of the two facing maidens. The figures' arms appear to support the horizontal of a cross, which shares a geometric pattern with the panel's borders. The figures are clothed in checkerboard- and triangle-linked robes that accentuate the verticality of the composition. The mosaic was designed to stand eight feet high but was never actualized.

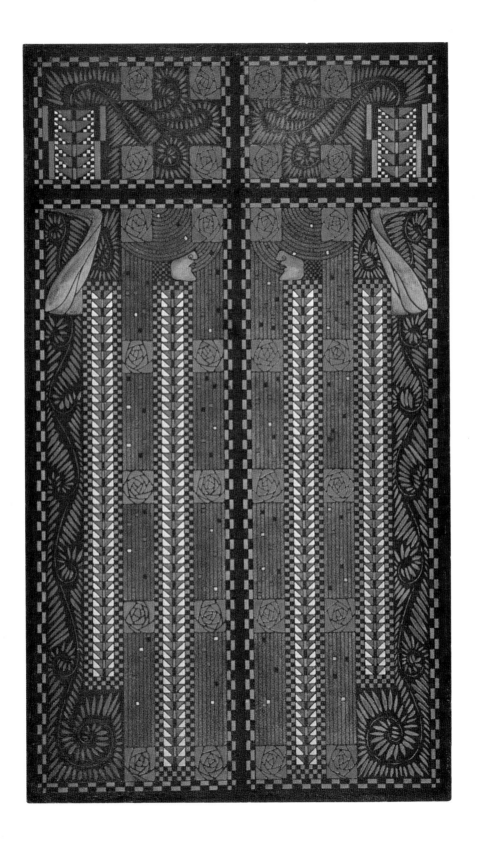

Appendix 1. Roycroft

This article by Dard Hunter, printed in the August 2, 1904, issue of the Chillicothe News-Advertiser, *presents his first impressions of the Roycroft community.*[*]

THE ROYCROFTERS
How the King Crafters Make Work a Pleasure Because They Are Artists and Make Beautiful Things

Seventeen miles west [*sic*] of Buffalo is a queer little village called East Aurora. This is where the Roycrofter cranks and their pastor, Elbert Hubbard, hang out. They are a settlement of peculiar thinking people who make useful and beautiful things as well as they can. They are called cranks by outsiders and perhaps they are cranks, for they are all original thinkers and work out original ideas. And these are the factors, as I understand, of the crank. These cranks are a good deal like the other cranks on the outside. They think all the rest of the world cranky because the rest of the world lacks the appreciation of the original thought and the original way of doing things.

Elbert Hubbard is probably the best known author in this country. "A Message to Garcia," is his best known book of which there were three million copies printed. This book had a powerful lesson in it, and this lesson has been taught and is taught here in the garden workshop, the workshop of artists—do your duty and do it well.

Mr. Hubbard not only thinks differently, but dresses differently, from others. He wears his curly black hair very long and a huge necktie adorns his neck. Most of the time he wears overalls but he himself is not an artisan, which is to say he does not work in the shop with his hands, but his brain does a great deal of the hardest work that is done here. He is one of the most noted and most popular Chautauqua lecturers in America; auditors like what he says and enjoy the manner of the saying.

Nearly all the Roycrofters allow their hair to grow and wear ties like the Fra. I have a big tie and I go bareheaded like all the others here. The ties cost a dollar each and are made by Roycroft girls seventy years young.

"John," as Mr. Hubbard is called up here, has three sons, Elbert, Ralph and Sanford. Sanford is known around these parts as "Sandy" or "Freckles." He is the most interesting of the three. Somebody asked him the other day what he did, and he replied that "he did as he damned pleased."

[*] From Hunter, Dard II. *The Life Work of Dard Hunter.* Vol. 1, pp. 12–17.

The Roycrofters have been in existence about nine years. They have five buildings of which they are very proud. They built them themselves. They are print shop, chapel, inn, blacksmith and cabinet-shops. All the buildings are surrounded by beautiful lawns, fruit trees, flower beds and things. There are tennis, croquet and handball courts where the toilers can amuse themselves at recess or after working hours. An old-fashioned well under the trees furnishes water to quench the thirst of the workers.

The print shop is of stone and is the larger building. Here is where the "Philistine," "Little Journeys" and all the books are printed, illuminated and bound. Rag carpet weaving and leather repoussé is also done in the print shop. It is a beautiful building, with its red tile roof, great wrought iron lanterns hanging over the oak doors, carved with ancient mottos. The inside is as handsome as the exterior. It is furnished in Roycroft furniture, the most beautiful because it is the simplest furniture, and is made by artists and not by mechanics and machines. It is solid and just what it appears to be—no shams, no veneer. It is good, plain, strong—artistic. The artists who make it use their brains and joy goes with the making. They make it because they like to create beauty and the creation delights them. Thus they are kings of craftsmen.

There are statuary, paintings and flowers in every room and pianos on every floor. The workers stop awhile now and then and play on the pianos or dance in the ball room. It's more like a palace than a factory. I should not say factory. It is not a factory. It is a place where artists work—where minds produce. The only machine in this artisan's palace is the hand of the artist driven by the artist's brain.

The chapel is where the Roycrofters find amusement nights. It's not a church as you would suppose but an art gallery. There are pedestals around supporting costly statues and the walls are hung with paintings, the works of Alexis Fournier, honest Roycrofter. In this chapel lectures and music are given nightly by the best talent. There is "no hold up at the door" either as Mr. Hubbard expresses it. Here services are held but not what you at Chillicothe would call religious services. There is music of the best and there are lectures not on Biblical subjects, but on art and artisans—lectures to inspire the worker, to show him the way to make beautiful things, to think beautiful thoughts, to do beautiful acts, and the directions of the teachers are followed in the shops, on the grounds, in every walk, in every action. There is inspiration in all of it for the artist-worker, whether he be painter, printer, cabinet maker or blacksmith.

Back of the print shop is the locksmith shop, where the hardware for the furniture, andirons and ornamental iron-works is wrought.

The blacksmith himself speaks three languages and is a thorough student of ancient history. He's a Socialist, and if you can get him to talk on any other subject you're a dandy. But this is not a Socialist community. It is a corporation and the men who work are paid as in any other private business enterprise.

A blacksmith shop is most always dingy, dark and dirty. This one isn't. Like the chapel and the print shop, it is made of rough stones picked up all over the country. The roof is of red tile and the walls are carved with vines. The inside is finished in yellow tinted plaster with a beautiful beamed ceiling. There's a big brick fire-place at one end with Roycroft andirons supporting huge logs ready to light when winter comes.

Right across the street is the "Phalansterie," the inn where the Roycrofters eat, drink and are merry.

The dining room is finished Roycroftie with huge round tables and the benches are logs split in half with legs driven into them. These benches are rather uncomfortable but what's the difference long as they are queer? There is a large carved sign hung on heavy chains in one end of the dining room which bears this motto:

Without the door
Let sorrow die;
And if perchance
It hap to die,
We'll bury it deep
In a Roycroft pie.

At the Phalanterier's back door is the cabinet-shop where such men as Uncle Albert [Danner], Deacon [Herbert] Buffum, Jim Cadzow and that bunch work.

Uncle Albert is the oldest—about seventy. He likes his tobacco and uses a good line of swear words but is there with the goods when it comes to handmade furniture.

The Roycrofters used to have a pottery where Sandy Hubbard made things out of clay. This has been torn down to make room for the new cabinet-shop. They also have two lumber camps, a saw-mill and potato patch.

The Roycrofters do an immense business. The printing monthly of the "Philistine" and "Little Journeys" with a hundred thousand copies each is no small task.

Every package sent from the Roycroft shop has an old rusty horse-shoe tied on it to assure that it will reach its destination safely.

Then there's Ali Baba too, the mascot of the Roycrofters. He is the old man who takes care of the horses and cows. He hangs out at the barn and can talk a blue streak.

The most beautiful books in the world are produced here. The illuminations and bindings are superb and the prices take one's breath.

They have here what is called a Roycroft summer school which is conducted in connection with the Roycroft shops. Bookbinding, drawing, illuminating, cabinet-making, outdoor sketching, gardening, type setting, French, German, Spanish, Italian, vocal and instrumental music, physical culture, English literature, and "right living through the exercise of the three H's—head, heart and hand" are taught.

There is a convention here of the American Academy of Immortals, and it costs $10 to be one. The membership fee entitles one to a subscription to the Philistine magazine for 99 years and a lot of other books that are worth the money. These Immortals have an annual dinner here this week, and will eat, drink and talk just like other folk and will have just as much fun: maybe more, for the object of these cranks is to make life beautiful for themselves as well as for others.

Dard Hunter at Roycroft, c. 1904–1905.
Photograph courtesy Richard Blacher.

Appendix 2.
Dard Hunter School of Handicraft

Dard Hunter's Make Arts-and-Crafts Things at Your Home *was a four-page pamphlet printed by the Roycroft Press in 1909 describing what the correspondent could make with instructions and tools Hunter would supply once the student enrolled in his course. The pamphlet text is reproduced here in full.*[*]

Most everybody is becoming more and more particular about the things they wear and place in their homes. Hand-made things are prized above everything: that is, things of an artistic or decorative purpose. All esthetic articles made by hand are constantly in demand. The machine-made thing is no longer appreciated.

Of the things made by hand, metal-work and leaded art-glass are perhaps the most desired. Metal-working includes jewelry and all things made in metal with an art intent. Wonderful effects can be produced by the use of metals and semi-precious stones. What is more beautiful than a hand-made buckle or watch-fob executed in silver and copper, set with a malachite or azurite! Or a jewel-box in copper with silver hinges tipped with corals! Then, too, larger things are made by hand in metal that are most effective and useful. Lamp-bases, nut bowls, paper-knives, trays and dozens of other articles combining the practical and artistic.

Working in leaded and stained glass is also most fascinating. This craft includes, mainly, the making of windows and lamp-shades. The use of opalescent glass of delicate coloring for shades, and lamp-bases made of copper, make, indeed, a handsome lighting fixture. Windows of any size, either in landscape or conventional designs can be used in any home. The same sash that held the old pane of glass can be used for the leaded panel.

Perhaps of all the crafts, these two—metal-work and leaded glass—are the most interesting. The reason these things have not been taken up by lovers of the arts and crafts, is because they have been unable to get the right kind of instruction.

Mr. Dard Hunter is devoting his life to arts and crafts. He has worked in the leading art shops of Europe, and is now foreman of the mechanical art department of The Roycroft Shop. Mr. Hunter's work includes these two most interesting crafts, metal-work and leaded glass. His work is entirely done by hand. He uses no machines. Mr. Hunter, with his experience, can enable you to make in your own home the things that he makes. He will give you instructions,

[*] From Baker, Cathleen A. *By His Own Labor: The Biography of Dard Hunter*, Oak Knoll Press, New Castle, Delaware, 2000, pp. 44–45.

all the tools needed, and materials too, if you desire. You can become a craftsman and craftswoman, without difficulty, with his help. His instructions are simple and easily understood.

Mr. Hunter has two branches of instruction, the jewelry and metal-working craft, and the making of art-glass windows and lamp-shades.

The metal-work instructions include the making of the most simple thing, up to difficult and skillful work. In the first lesson you are given something to do—perhaps a buckle or watch-fob to make in silver and copper. There is no tedious working before you begin to make something; you will be interested from the very start. The instructions are all plain and practical. There is nothing left for you to wonder about. All kinds of soldering, setting of stones, and in fact, everything pertaining to the making of modern hand-made jewelry and metal-work is clearly taught. If you at any time have difficulty you are at liberty to send your work to Mr. Hunter for advice. He will tell you just what is needed. Perhaps he will fix it himself and return it to you.

The leaded art-glass instructions include everything connected with the making of windows and lamp-shades. In this work, as in the metal course, the worker is given something to do from the beginning. The first lesson is making a leaded glass window in a conventional design. One that can be used in your home, as it can be made any size.

Pattern-making, the cutting of glass, leading, soldering, cementing and everything needful in the work is thoroughly treated.

The making of these things can be accomplished in your own home during your spare time. You will be surprised how quickly you "take hold."

The materials used are very inexpensive. The metal required for a piece of jewelry would amount to only a few cents. Glass and lead for window and shade mats sell at fifteen cents a pound. All designs needed are furnished with instructions.

This arts-and-crafts work is entirely suited to ladies and can be taken up by them as readily as by men.

The course in either craft extends over an indefinite period, owing to the length of time the worker has at disposal. The price for either the metal-work course or the leaded art-glass course is $15.00, or $25.00 for both. This includes all tools needed. Don't you think you'd like to make arts-and-crafts things?

Selected Bibliography

Baker, Cathleen A. *By His Own Labor: The Biography of Dard Hunter*. New Castle, Delaware: Oak Knoll Press, 2000.

———. "The Lonhuda Art Pottery at Steubenville," *Style 1900*, vol. 12, no. 2 (Spring 1999).

———. "Sleuthing for Dard Hunter in Vienna," *Craftsman Homeowner*, vol. 6, no. 1 (Winter 1994). Foundation for the Study of the Arts & Crafts Movement at Roycroft.

Dard Hunter Archives at Mountain House, Chillicothe, Ohio.

Hamilton, Charles. *As Bees in Honey Drown: The Loves, Lives and Letters of The Roycroft's Alice and Elbert Hubbard*. Tavares, Florida: SPS Publications, 1997.

Hunter, Dard. *Make Arts-and-Crafts Things at Your Home* (four-page leaflet). East Aurora, New York, 1909.

———. *My Life with Paper: An Autobiography*. New York: Alfred A. Knopf, 1958.

———. *Papermaking: The History and Technique of an Ancient Craft*. New York: Dover Publications, 1978. First published 1943 by A. A. Knopf.

Hunter, Dard II. *The Life Work of Dard Hunter*. 2 vols. Chillicothe, Ohio: Mountain House Press, 1981, 1983.

Kreisman, Lawrence, "Discovering Secession Vienna," *Style 1900*, vol. 23, no. 3 (Fall 2010), 68–75.

Postcards of the Wiener Werkstätte: A Catalogue Raisonné: Selections from The Leonard A. Lauder Collection. Edited by Elisabeth Schmuttermeier and Christian Witt-Dörring. New York: Neue Galerie, 2010.

Shay, Felix. *Elbert Hubbard of East Aurora*. New York: Wm. H. Wise & Co., 1926.

Via, Maria, and Marjorie Searl. *Head, Heart and Hand: Elbert Hubbard and the Roycrofters*. Rochester, New York: University of Rochester Press, 1994.

JOURNALS AND PERIODICALS

Dekorative Kunst

Deutsche Kunst und Dekoration

Die Kunst

The Studio

Index